INTERNATIONAL ACCOUNTING STANDARDS versus US-GAAP REPORTING: Empirical Evidence Based On Case Studies

Trevor S. Harris
Kester and Byrnes Professor of Accounting
Columbia Business School
Columbia University

SOUTH-WESTERN College Publishing

An International Thomson Publishing Company

Sponsoring Editor: Elizabeth A. Bowers
Production Editor: Peggy A. Williams
Production House: DPS Associates, Inc.
Cover Designer: Rick Moore
Marketing Manager: Sharon C. Oblinger

ISBN: 0-538-85693-9

1 2 3 4 5 6 7 MT 1 0 9 8 7 6 5

Printed in the United States of America

I(T)P
International Thomson Publishing

South-Western College Publishing is an ITP Company. The ITP trademark is used under license.

Dedicated to Michele and Sylvia for their encouragement and support.

Acknowledgments

I am grateful to Coopers & Lybrand L.L.P. for their extensive support. Particular thanks are due to Ronald Murray and Jeffrey Hoover for providing so much effort in and support to the project. I also thank the members of Coopers & Lybrand's International Task Force, Martin Aked, Paul Cherry, Sigvard Heurlin, Ronald Murray, Douglas Paterson, and Michael Sharpe; and other Coopers and Lybrand L.L.P. personnel who assisted in various ways. This includes Nelson Dittmar, Richard Fuchs, Mike Lofing, Geoff Manger, David Randell, Bernard Rascle, Pierre Riou, Scott Robinson, Timothy Robinson, Robert Singer, George Starr, Lyle Steidinger, Dennis Svensson, Lee Ann Underwood, and Jonathan Wood. Coopers & Lybrand L.L.P.'s professional technical support has been beneficial to this project. Nevertheless, the commentary and opinions within this book are those of the author.

Special thanks are due to Jean-Pierre Wirtz of Holderbank, who helped with the conception of, and initial impetus for the project, and to the other senior managers of the participating companies. These managers include: Piero Bonardi, Rolf Fischer, Christian Gabrillagues, Michael Gillian, Pascal Giraud, Hans Lindblad, Bernd-Joachim Menn, Bill Volum, and Shane Warbrick.

Part of the research and most of the writing of this project was undertaken while working at Salomon Brothers Inc and I appreciate their support, especially the assistance of Doris Barba and Evelyn Pepi, who assisted with the typing of this monograph.

I also received support from the Rudolph Schoenheimer Fellowship, the Center on International Business Education and Research and the Jerome A. Chazen Institute of International Business at Columbia Business School.

All of these colleagues are not responsible for errors or omissions. Further, although I am a representative on the Consultative Group of the IASC, this should not be taken to mean that the IASC necessarily agrees with the opinions contained herein.

Thanks also go to Mark Hubble, Elizabeth Bowers, and Peggy Williams of South-Western Publishing for their tolerance and help in the quick turnaround of this monograph.

The most essential ingredient for the completion of the project has been the tolerance and unending support of my wife Michele to whom I am eternally grateful.

All inferences, conclusions and errors remain the responsibility of the author.

Contents

1

INTRODUCTION

As globalization of business activity and financial markets proceeds at a rapid pace, a desire for a single set of accounting standards has been expressed frequently (Liener [1994]). Given differing institutional settings in many countries, especially in such critical areas as corporate governance, legal structure, taxation, and capital market development, it is implausible to suggest that a single financial reporting system can evolve which is adequate for all companies in every setting. Nevertheless, there are a number of companies that operate in a manner that transcends idiosyncratic national characteristics, and that actively seek capital in international financial markets. For these companies, it is plausible that a single set of accounting standards may be adequate to satisfy investor needs, in particular if such international standards are supplemented with local rules dealing with specific national issues and a strict enforcement mechanism.

This broad concept has been the basic objective of the International Accounting Standards Committee [IASC] since its inception in 1973. Critics of the International Accounting Standards [IAS] issued by the IASC argue that they are the product of a political compromise and therefore are largely unconstrained, achieving the status of the "lowest common denominator." On the other hand, United States Generally Accepted Accounting Principles [US-GAAP] are viewed by many as the appropriate benchmark for high-quality financial reporting standards.[1] An obvious question that arises is: How different would the financial reporting be if companies applied IAS instead of US-GAAP? This monograph addresses this question for non-US companies by undertaking a detailed analysis of several companies as if each company complied with the current requirements for non-US companies registering with the United States Securities and Exchange Commission [SEC] for the purposes of listing on a US securities exchange.

---

1 For example, in a letter to the SEC dated June 30, 1994, the Financial Accounting Policies Committee of the Association for Investment Management and Research states "The FAPC believes that the current U.S. reporting and disclosure system is the best in the world." See also Breeden [1994].

A key sub-question to be considered is: Why should IAS not be acceptable for firms listing on a US exchange? This question is addressed because the SEC currently requires all non-US registrants to reconcile their financial statements to US-GAAP; a requirement that has been viewed as a major constraint to some companies listing their shares in the US.[2] Nevertheless, the evidence presented should be informative for other jurisdictions outside of the US as it provides direct evidence of the information provided under IAS relative to practices within sample firms' countries and relative to a widely known and respected benchmark. It is hoped that the evidence will facilitate informed decision making in the continuing evaluation of financial reporting for those entities demanding international capital.

The analysis demonstrates that companies that comply with the **revised IAS** provide accounting measures that are essentially consistent with US-GAAP, and, where they differ, it seems difficult to argue that use of IAS will compromise the relevance of the data. Differences arise in certain key areas. Two of these are accounting for business combinations and foreign currency translation. In both instances, there is no compelling evidence why US-GAAP is superior to IAS. The Financial Accounting Standards Board [FASB] and other standard setters (for example, the Accounting Standards Board of the United Kingdom [UK]) have business combinations on their agendas suggesting some concern with existing practice in this area. In addition, in December 1994, the SEC accepted key elements of the two relevant IAS for non-US registrants.[3]

One current concern with IAS is that there are areas in which an IAS does not exist. In some of these cases, the IASC has the issue under consideration but has not completed its standard-setting process. In other cases, the issue is not yet under formal consideration. Realistically, these areas must continue to fall under a local regulatory authority, at least until the IAS has a standard. This is analogous to the situation in the US where the SEC may choose to adopt an accounting practice even in an area in which the FASB has no standard in place. The concluding chapter proposes a system that allows IAS as the benchmark while maintaining the integrity and quality of the US financial reporting system.

The discussions with sample companies revealed several differences between individual country practices and both IAS and US-GAAP. Several of these differences reflect institutional variations, many of which are of a historic nature and apply more to tightly held national companies with little, or at least diminishing, relevance for the multinational corporations seeking foreign listings. For companies and countries willing to focus on reporting the economic substance of transactions and business activity, it is apparent that where IAS

---

2 This issue is discussed in many papers. Recent examples include: Fuerbringer [1992], Amir, Harris and Venuti [1993], Barth and Clinch [1994], Breeden [1994], Cochrane [1994], Decker [1994], and Harris, Lang and Möller [1994].
3 See SEC Release Nos 33-7117, 33-7119, 34-35093, 34-35095.

exist **and companies comply with them**, they provide equivalent—if not superior—data as compared to data arising from any national set of standards.

One of the most disturbing features observed was a growing tendency to focus on conforming to narrowly defined measurement rules that did not necessarily reflect the economic substance of transactions. This phenomenon exists in most jurisdictions and is unquestionably apparent in the US; in the FASB standards, the standards created by other policy-making bodies such as the Emerging Issues Task Force (EITF), and the staff rulings of the SEC.[4] We conjecture that this narrow focus has arisen in the US as a result of imposing comparability as a primary objective and a perception that managers take maximum liberty in using accounting to exploit information asymmetries. The demand for narrowly defined measurement rules may also result from a perception that this aids the accountants' defense in the aggressively litigious environment that exists today. While judgments cannot be placed on the veracity of these beliefs in an international setting, the evidence suggests that there are many examples where more detailed rules, as opposed to a broader rule that has the same basic requirements, has NOT eliminated (or even reduced) the opportunity for abuse. The evidence further suggests that the detailed rules have created an illusion of precision in accounting measures that by their nature result from subjective choices. Hence, one must wonder whether such detailed measurement rules have exacerbated litigation rather than reduced it.

Readers of this report are urged to consider the questions and findings from a constructive perspective and consider what it would take to have IAS work, rather than to try and find each element of IAS that may be incomplete relative to existing (idiosyncratic) practices.

The monograph proceeds as follows. Chapter 2 describes the approach taken in performing the analysis and provides a brief description of the companies included in the study. Chapter 3 summarizes the results of the analysis. Chapter 4 presents conclusions and suggests some recommendations and challenges to regulators, companies, the accounting profession, and the IASC. Appendices contain a more detailed description of IAS and how these differ from US-GAAP for non-US registrants, and a detailed summary of the analysis of the financial statements for each company. The company analyses cover all differences and, where feasible, provide a detailed reconciliation of shareholders' equity to US-GAAP, as required by the SEC for non-US registrants.

---

4 See also the recent report by the Advisory Panel on Auditor Independence *Strengthening the Professionalism of the Independent Auditor* [1994] for a similar view, for example pages 5 and 6.

2

NATURE OF ANALYSIS
AND SAMPLE SELECTION

2.1 BACKGROUND

The project was conceived in March 1993, at the time that Daimler-Benz announced it was to list on the New York Stock Exchange [NYSE]. Preceding the announcement, a team of external advisors and the firm's personnel had analyzed what adjustments would be necessary to move from German GAAP to US-GAAP. Having discussed the process with Jean-Pierre Wirtz of Holderbank, a large Swiss cement group applying IAS, I agreed that it would be interesting to perform a similar exercise for Holderbank and other companies. The objective of the proposed exercise was to evaluate the extent to which IAS differ from US-GAAP with respect to the requirements imposed on non-US registrants by the SEC.

As discussed in Chapter 1, the research is motivated by the well-documented perception that many non-US companies choose not to list on a US stock exchange because of an unwillingness to perform the reconciliation to US-GAAP required by current US regulation. While it is difficult to obtain irrefutable evidence that the reconciliation requirement is the reason a number of companies avoid listing on a US exchange, the growth in both the Electronic Bulletin Board or "pink sheet" and the Rule 144a private placement markets (Edwards [1992]; Greene, Braverman, and Sperber [1994]; Velli [1994]) attest to the likelihood of the phenomenon. In particular, as Greene et al [1994] observe, the prospectuses for Rule 144a placements contain most of the information for a registered offering on a stock exchange with the usual exception of the US-GAAP reconciliations. A second concern, alluded to by German companies in their request to avoid the SEC's reconciliation requirements, is the potential confusion raised by the disclosure of more than one earnings or shareholders' equity measure (Harris, Lang, and Möller [1994]; Liener [1994]).

One option would be for each country to accept other countries' reporting systems and let investors decide what they find acceptable. This process is occurring indirectly as investors move their funds into other national markets. However, given the political realities and existing suspicions, it seems unlikely that the SEC, or non-US regulators, will accept the reporting systems of other countries in the foreseeable future. Even the mutual recognition agreement between the US and Canada still requires reconciliation of the primary accounting measures for certain types of capital-raising issues. Hence, a feasible option in the near term is to have a financial reporting system that meets the concerns of global investors and the various national regulators interested in protecting their constituent investors. This might be achieved by the regulators of the various jurisdictions creating an umbrella body similar to those for other social and economic issues. While some steps have clearly been taken in this direction, they are at their early stages. However, the IASC had begun a process of establishing globally accepted standards more than twenty years ago. While critics have argued that these standards are broad and work to the lowest common denominator as part of the process of compromise, there seems to be no empirical evidence as to whether such a claim is valid.

In essence, this was the question that evolved from the process begun with Daimler-Benz's attempt to understand how easily it could comply with US-GAAP: If a global company applied IAS, how different would the measures be from US-GAAP as required of non-US registrants for registering with the SEC and listing on a US stock exchange? It is to be emphasized from the outset that the objective considered as the primary benchmark is "the pursuit of investor protection through transparent financial reporting and full and complete disclosure" (Breeden [1994]). As the IASC has recently completed its "improvements project," which was aimed at minimizing the set of choices available in IAS, the revised standards have been used as the benchmark for comparison to US-GAAP.

At the time the project was being conceived, a conversation was held with Ronald J. Murray, an IASC Board Member for the US at that time and National Director of Accounting and SEC Services at Coopers & Lybrand L.L.P. He and his partners on Coopers & Lybrand's International Accounting Task Force agreed to sponsor and participate in the project. Mr. Murray agreed to help identify candidate companies from a set of countries and have a Coopers & Lybrand L.L.P. partner participate in each meeting to facilitate the evaluation and to ensure a "quality control" of the analysis. One objective in selecting companies was to try to ensure that a cross-section of countries and industries was covered. But, given the expense both in time and financial cost for each visit, there was a limit to the number of observations that could be obtained. Furthermore, as each company had to volunteer to be a part of this project, the potential for a self-selection bias obviously remains. Consequently, the reader should be cautious about presuming that these findings can be generalized to all companies applying IAS. Nevertheless, as any reading of a cross-section of US annual reports will reveal, it would be naive to presume that all US corporations apply US-GAAP in a uniform manner. Furthermore, it is suggested that, if a set of companies complying with IAS reveals an acceptable level of reporting, then any potential concerns about a more general application would have to relate to conformity and compliance, rather than to the standards themselves.

2.2 THE PROCESS

The specific process followed was:

1. Several companies were approached either by the author or a partner of Coopers & Lybrand L.L.P. The approaches were made to various clients or personal contacts. Of the eight companies that agreed to participate, five were Coopers & Lybrand L.L.P. audit clients and three were not. One of the three companies appointed Coopers & Lybrand as joint auditors in 1994. To ensure that a breadth of countries was covered, only one company in any country was actively recruited. No country was excluded deliberately.
2. Once a company agreed to participate, the author and a partner of Coopers & Lybrand L.L.P., knowledgeable about US-GAAP and SEC practices, spent one to two days with the company. The most recent annual report of the company had been carefully analyzed prior to the meeting and each line item of the financial statements and all disclosures were evaluated to ensure conformity with the requirements of completing the financial accounting section of a US registration under Item 18 of Form 20-F. In some cases, the sample firm already applied IAS; in others, the IAS were either partially applied or were under consideration. Where the company did not yet apply IAS as revised, the first step was to evaluate the adjustments to revised IAS and then from IAS to US-GAAP. Focus was placed on the measurement questions because of the frequent debate about the reconciliations required for non-US registrants. However, the issues relating to disclosures were also noted. In each case, analysis was made of the company's treatment with the equivalent of the chief financial officer and/or the controller/chief accounting officer responsible for group reporting purposes. In most cases, where relevant, the person responsible for group consolidation also participated in the meetings.
3. At the conclusion of the initial analysis and meeting with the company, a report was written summarizing the findings and detailing the issues for which points remained open. This report was sent to the management of the companies to verify the facts and in most cases to undertake additional work required to obtain any missing or incomplete data.
4. Simultaneously, Jeff Hoover, a Coopers & Lybrand L.L.P. partner acting as the key liaison person for the project, together with a team of managers, undertook a review of the case studies and findings based on their independent reading of each annual report in terms of its compliance with US-GAAP. This procedure led to a set of detailed working papers that

acted as a backup check on the analysis. Any further outstanding points
were then resubmitted to the local liaison and relevant companies.
5. Finally, the draft of this report was submitted to the companies and the participating liaison partners as a final check on the validity of the technical
information.

In all cases where the data were not in the annual report, the primary source
of information for the additional data was the ledgers or working papers from
the immediately preceding set of audited financial statements. In some cases,
the firms had to go back to the subsidiaries to gather the data. Hence, the managers of each company were responsible for the veracity of the information as
none of the additional information gleaned was specifically audited. But it is
emphasized that in most cases (for example, the reconstitution of the goodwill
measures), this analysis is based on data the company had taken from working
papers that had already been audited. Furthermore, as each participating company had the right to maintain complete anonymity, there is little direct incentive
for them to provide misleading information.

2.3 THE SAMPLE OF FIRMS

Table 1 provides some descriptive information about each participating company. The sample of eight companies covers seven countries: Australia, France
(2), Germany, Italy, New Zealand, Sweden, and Switzerland. The companies
operate in varying industries including automotive components, building products, cement, chemicals, heavy and light engineering equipment, information
technology, mining, pharmaceuticals, and pulp and paper products.

The entities differ in size with revenues ranging from US dollar equivalents of $2.2 billion to $25.5 billion. Income varies from a loss of $442 million to
income of $888 million, although for many of the companies the earnings in the
test year were depressed by the broad recession in the US and other industrialized economies.

The fiscal year-ends were in 1992 or 1993 as the analysis took place over
more than one year. The analysis and inferences are based on the annual reports most current at the time of our visit. In many cases, the data and/or
disclosures may differ from the financial statements provided in later periods,
as the reporting practices of companies continue to evolve over time. This analysis considers primarily the US-GAAP practices required at the time the financial
statements were prepared. However, certain implications of this restriction are
discussed in some of the detailed descriptions and in the conclusion.

Half of the companies had a small number of shareholders with large holdings, although in all cases there was widespread share ownership for the shares
in public float. Two of the companies are already listed on the NYSE. Two other
sample firms had prepared US-GAAP reconciliations for investors with more

than a 20 percent ownership. For one of these companies, the reconciliation had been performed in the sample period while for the other the reconciliation was a couple of years old as the investor requiring US-GAAP no longer held a sufficient number of shares to require equity accounting. Hence, audited US-GAAP data were available for half the sample.

None of the other companies anticipated listing on a US securities exchange within a year of our visit although each company considered such a listing as a possibility at some point in the future.

While the sample of firms may not be ideal in terms of covering all major industrialized countries or all industries, it is believed the sample represents a sufficient cross-section of each factor to provide useful insights.

Table 1   Descriptive Information About Sample Companies

TABLE 1
Descriptive Information About Sample Companies

Company	Country of Incorporation	Key Industries	Basis of Group Accounting	Fiscal Year Used For Study	Gross Revenue (Millions)	Reported Earnings[1] (Millions)	Reported Equity[1] (Millions)
Atlas Copco	Sweden	Compressor, construction and mining, and industrial techniques	Swedish GAAP	1992	SEK 16,007 (US$ 2,277)	SEK 604 (US$ 86)	SEK 7,295 (US$ 1,038)
Bayer	Germany	Chemical, pharmaceutical	German GAAP	1993	DM 41,007 (US$ 25,470)	DM 1,327 (US$ 824)	DM 17,681 (US$ 10,982)
Broken Hill Proprietary Company	Australia	Mining, petroleum and steel	Australian GAAP[2]	1993	A$ 15,934 (US$ 10,934)	A$ 1,294 (US$ 888)	A$ 8,867 (US$ 6,085)
Cap Gemini Sogeti	France	Consulting and information technology services	IAS (Unrevised)	1992	FF 11,884 (US$ 2,152)	FF (72) (US$ (13))	FF 5,179 (US$ 938)
Fletcher Challenge	New Zealand	Pulp and paper, building materials and energy	New Zealand GAAP[2]	1993	NZ $9,486 (US$ 5,108)	NZ $382 (US$ 206)	NZ$4,456 (US$ 2,400)
Holderbank	Switzerland	Cement and building materials	IAS	1992	SFr 7,836 (US$ 5,367)	SFr 136 (US$ 93)	SFr 3,005 (US$ 2,059)
Olivetti	Italy	Information technology	Italian GAAP and IAS (unrevised)	1992	IL 8,025,465 (US$ 5,456)	IL (649,853) (US$ (442))	IL 2,361,188 (US$ 1,605)
Valeo	France	Automotive components	IAS (unrevised)	1992	FF 20,645 (US$ 3,738)	FF 700 (US$ 127)	FF 7,213 (US$ 1,306)

1 Earnings and shareholders' equity exclude minority interest.
2 Registered with the SEC and hence provides supplementary information in conformity with US-GAAP.

3

RESULTS OF ANALYSIS

3.1 INTRODUCTION

The results are presented in three forms. First, the results are described and classified by the key accounting practices. Second, Tables 2 and 3 summarize the difference for each sample company for the accounting practices that were found to have a significant difference in the detailed analysis.[1] The deviations are differentiated both between the company's practice and revised IAS, and revised IAS and US-GAAP. Table 2 provides a brief descriptive summary while Table 3 provides the reconciliation to shareholders' equity for the fiscal year studied. Finally, Appendix B provides a description of the same basic information on a case (company) specific basis.

3.2 SPECIFIC DIFFERENCES

The specific differences are considered under thirteen different categories. The prose discusses the overall nature of each of the differences and alludes to the individual case studies. Readers interested in a particular company should refer to the detailed description in Appendix B or the summary data in Tables 2 and 3. A reconciliation to shareholders' equity and not earnings is provided because only one year of data was verified. Further, as discussed and shown in Amir, Harris, and Venuti [1993], the shareholders' equity reconciliations generally provide the primary source of information content from Form 20-F reconciliations.[2]

---

1 In a few cases, we report differences that are immaterial to indicate that a potentially relevant issue was considered. For example, if a reconciliation to US-GAAP was published we do not want to exclude items included in such a reconciliation.

2 Barth and Clinch [1994] using an alternate methodology and smaller sample argue that there is some information content in earnings reconciliations.

The categories described cover the areas in which differences were found in more than one case. There is no particular order to the categories but the most material differences occurred in five areas: acquisitions, business combinations, and consolidations; foreign currency translation; post-employment benefits; property, plant, and equipment; and taxation. This finding is consistent with Amir, Harris, and Venuti [1993].

3.2.A. ACQUISITIONS, BUSINESS COMBINATIONS, AND CONSOLIDATIONS

This category covers areas in accounting that are currently the focus of attention by accounting standard-setters in several countries, including the US and UK. The primary issues concern the scope of group reporting and accounting for goodwill (premium on acquisition).

Current US-GAAP requires consolidation of all subsidiaries and equity accounting for investees over which the investor has significant influence. At the date of acquisition, the transaction is accounted for as either a "pooling of interest" or a "purchase." In the latter case, the difference between the purchase price and the fair value of net assets acquired is capitalized as an asset (goodwill) and amortized over the expected economic life with a maximum amortization period of 40 years, a period chosen frequently by companies applying US-GAAP. Recently, the SEC has been taking a closer look at the amortization period chosen and any impairment in the value of goodwill.

Revised IAS requires full consolidation of all subsidiaries with a more restrictive set of conditions (relative to US-GAAP) under which pooling ("uniting") of interest must be used. Goodwill must be capitalized and amortized over its expected useful life with a maximum amortization period of 20 years. IAS 22 also requires an annual evaluation of the value of goodwill. Under IAS, equity accounting must be used for associated companies except for certain joint ventures for which the benchmark treatment is proportional consolidation, with the US-GAAP requirement of equity accounting an allowed alternative. In November 1993, the SEC adopted rules that permitted non-US registrants to use proportional consolidation for joint ventures.

Differences found in the specific cases included: the allocation of goodwill to an asset "market share," which is not amortized; a specific application of pooling of interest; the exclusion of equity accounting from the primary financial statements; and the treatment of an associate company's value of equity prior to increased investment by the investor. For all these issues, IAS and US-GAAP are consistent, so that adjustment to revised IAS would achieve the goal of conformity.

Given the apparent similarity between US-GAAP and revised IAS in this category, it may seem surprising that business combinations and goodwill remains an area in which material differences exist. The primary reason is that, under revised IAS, retroactive adjustments for changes in accounting policies to conform with the revised standard are not required. So in all but one case where there is an adjustment to shareholders' equity (and earnings), when moving from revised IAS to US-GAAP, relating to the category of business combinations, no reconciliation is required beyond the retroactive adjustments. The one additional reconciliation item related to the treatment of net operating loss carryforwards of an acquiree for which IAS is currently silent.

Accounting for goodwill has often been cited as an area of competitive advantage for some countries relative to others (Choi and Lee [1991]). Global adoption of revised IAS 22 will eliminate any such situation. In a move in this direction, in December 1994, the SEC accepted certain provisions of IAS 22 for non-US registrants. Nevertheless, as the economic environment evolves into a more complex set of interactions and alliances across companies and regions, it is anticipated that this area of accounting will see constant reevaluation and change. Many such issues are currently being debated in several countries, including the US and the UK, with relatively recent changes in the European Union and several Asian countries. Furthermore, within each country, including the US, companies are choosing different approaches to accounting for business combinations and goodwill. In part as a result of the lack of comparability associated with goodwill recognition, a recent report by the Association for Investment Management and Research argued against capitalization of goodwill (Knutson [1993], page 49). Consequently, if one is concerned with investors' interests, it is not clear what argument can be made against measurements based on IAS, relative to US-GAAP, in this category.

3.2.B. FOREIGN CURRENCY TRANSLATION

US-GAAP has been through several iterations in the development of practice in this area. At present, the key standard is SFAS 52, which was a replacement of the highly controversial SFAS 8. SFAS 52 was itself quite controversial, with its acceptance based on a 4 to 3 vote by the FASB members at the time.

The revised IAS 21, which covers this topic, has requirements that largely mirror SFAS 52. A potentially material difference found in several cases exists with respect to the treatment of subsidiaries operating in hyperinflationary economies. Where these subsidiaries are not considered separate operating entities (in a specific currency), IAS 21 requires a price-level adjustment of the local currency balances before translation into the reporting currency and incorporation into the consolidated financial statements. At the time of the analysis, it was understood that the SEC interpreted SFAS 52 such that a subsidiary operating in, for example, Brazil, and invoicing its products in local currency (cruzeiro or real), had to use the reporting currency as the functional currency. Consequently, the sample companies that view the US dollar as the economically realistic operating currency, and so adopt it as the functional currency for their Brazilian subsidiaries, would have to remeasure these operations in the reporting currency. So, in the case of Holderbank, this practice would require a remeasurement from US dollars into Swiss francs.

Similarly, at that time, a company applying IAS 21 and restating the local currency statements prior to translation would have to use an approach with the reporting currency as the functional currency.

These practices, imposed on non-US registrants, are judged to be contrary to economic substance and to be a questionable interpretation of SFAS 52. But what makes the practice even more puzzling is that Items 17 and 18 of Form 20-F allow that same Brazilian subsidiary to use the local inflation-adjusted accounts as the basis of its own financial statements as a SEC registrant.[3]

Possibly recognizing the inconsistent nature of its US practice, in December 1994, the SEC accepted IAS 21 for the treatment of subsidiaries operating in hyperinflationary economies for non-US registrants. Despite this issue representing a clear difference at the time of the study, the adjustment to US-GAAP for this difference was not quantified as it was not considered to be a useful exercise given the high costs that would be involved, and given the SEC's proposal in mid-1994.

Revised IAS 21 excluded the required treatment for hedging under the presumption that the topic would be covered in the Financial Instruments project (E40 and then E48). That project has been suffering long delays, not dissimilar to the experience in several other countries, including the US. US-GAAP has an inconsistent treatment for foreign currency and other financial instruments while the FASB follows its course of standard development (Herz [1994]). Nevertheless, currently IAS is silent on hedging of foreign currency items so that a serious gap exists relative to US-GAAP.

A final difference found in one of the sample companies relates to an option in IAS to adjust the cost of an asset by a related exchange loss arising from a severe devaluation of a currency against which there is no practical means of hedging. This treatment is not allowed under US-GAAP and is likely to occur rarely.

3.2.C. SHAREHOLDERS' EQUITY

Several specific differences were found under this category, for which IAS are relatively sparse. In particular, differences between company practices and US-GAAP were found in: the treatment of employee stock options—an area where US-GAAP is evolving amidst significant controversy (Beese [1994]); the allocation to equity of the implied value of detachable warrants in a debt issue; and, the treatment of proposed dividends as a reduction of equity before legally declared, which is allowed as an alternative treatment under IAS.

---

3 For example, in its Form 20-F, Aracruz Cellulosa, a Brazilian company listed on the New York Stock Exchange, includes price-level-adjusted cruzeiro (real) accounts, as well as condensed financial statements based on a US dollar as functional currency approach. Conceivably, neither of these methods could have been used if Aracruz was a subsidiary of a non-US registrant and the SEC imposed its interpretation of US-GAAP.

Many non-US companies view financial reporting from an entity perspective rather than a proprietary (holding company shareholder) perspective, which is the usual basis in the US. Consequently, minority shareholders' interest is frequently included in total shareholders' equity. Given that the minority interests are always separately disclosed on the financial statements, it is believed that, from a users' perspective, this treatment leads to a reclassification item (rather than a reconciling measurement difference) under IAS and US-GAAP. This reclassification would be required for several of the companies.

The question of what to do where IAS is silent and US-GAAP exists is addressed in the conclusion.

3.2.D. PROPERTY, PLANT, AND EQUIPMENT [PP&E]

Several individual topics fall within this broad category. US-GAAP requires a strict application of historical cost for PP&E. Historical cost is the benchmark treatment under IAS, but an allowed alternative is the use of revalued amounts (less accumulated depreciation) for PP&E. If the allowed alternative is used, then the company is required to revalue the class of assets regularly to ensure they are reflected at fair value.

Many countries allow or require revaluations of PP&E, and the sample included several instances where revaluation had occurred in the past. Given the SEC's objective of ensuring investor protection, a critical question to ask is whether the revaluations are value-relevant to investors. In a comprehensive study, Easton, Eddey, and Harris [1993] analyzed this question for revaluations of PP&E in the Australian market. They found that revaluations in Australia were in fact value-relevant. Amir, Harris, and Venuti [1993] came to a similar conclusion for their comprehensive sample of non-US registrants. Barth and Clinch [1994], focusing separately on Australian and UK companies registered with the SEC, found that while the results for the Australian companies are consistent with the other studies, the value-relevance of UK revaluations (for current US registrants) is unclear. This result is perceived to be because UK companies use revaluations in a more ad hoc and strategic manner. If this perception is correct, the practice would be obviated by enforcement of the revised IAS, which requires regular revaluation. Furthermore, revised IAS requires disclosure of the historical cost carrying-value when a revaluation policy is used. The sample companies that had revalued assets did not perform revaluations on a regular basis, and so would not meet the requirements of the allowed alternative of the revised IAS 16.

A second subtopic to consider is capitalization of interest (borrowing costs). US-GAAP requires capitalization of interest under certain conditions. IAS 23 (as revised) allows for capitalization of borrowing costs under similar conditions to those in US-GAAP, but this is the allowed alternative treatment. The benchmark treatment under IAS is to expense all borrowing costs in the period incurred. This standard provides a good example of how a non-US firm can adopt IAS and either choose to be consistent with US-GAAP, or not, depending on the specific option it adopts. In the sample, two companies would have been required to provide a reconciling item for interest capitalization, although, in both cases, the reconciling item for US-GAAP purposes was to capture the retroactive effect of the new policy. The debate surrounding capitalization of borrowing costs reflects a common conflict between the traditional concepts of conservatism and matching. As there is currently no clear theoretical answer to such debates, the FASB chose a route of capitalization while the IASC accepted the two alternatives as being valid. Consequently, the topic provides a useful illustration for assessing the question as to whether allowing alternatives when the conceptual answer is unclear is a poor choice. Readers will naturally differ in their answers.

The third subtopic under the PP&E heading is capitalization of research and development costs. The sample included a couple of examples in which company practice differed from US-GAAP and in one case also IAS. Both sets of standards require that all research costs and internally generated software be expensed. Under specific conditions, IAS requires capitalization of certain development costs that would be expensed under US-GAAP. So, in this instance, IAS takes a less conservative route than US-GAAP, which is in contrast to the interest capitalization case.

A final area covered is accounting for leases. While there were some differences in the disclosures, there were no cases in which leases qualifying for capitalization under US-GAAP did not also qualify as such under IAS. The leasing area appears to be a classic, and extreme, example of how a simple statement of the basic principles, as in IAS 17, can provide equivalent information for investors to the information from the much more detailed and complex array of standards and technical interpretations found in US-GAAP.

In sum, the area of PP&E illustrates differences between IAS and US-GAAP in which honest purveyors of accounting relevance can choose to differ, and the result will always be subject to debate. The question remains whether investors' interests are necessarily compromised by adopting IAS in this area. It is difficult to conceive why this would be so.

3.2.E INVESTMENTS

Accounting policies for investments, incorporating the area of financial instruments in general, are evolving and have been the focus of much attention by accounting standard-setters. Since the time the tests were performed, US-GAAP has been refined and has required much more disclosure than is required by IAS and probably most other national standards. Consequently, if the analyses were performed today there might be even more differences to report, especially as it has proven difficult to get the proposed IAS [E48] accepted by the Board of the IASC.

The measurement differences related to the application of various adjustments to market value. Nevertheless, while the measurement differences were little, the disclosure differences were potentially significant.

This area illustrates two important points. First, the measurement issues that have been the focus of so much public debate, because of the necessity to report more than one earnings measure, obscure the discussion of the disclosure differences that may exist. Second, measurement differences are most apparent where IAS has not yet evolved.

3.2.F.   DISCONTINUED OPERATIONS AND CHANGES IN ACCOUNTING POLICIES

As indicated, adoption of the revised IAS does not require retroactive adjustment. As a result, within several categories reconciling items were found between revised IAS and US-GAAP, which are reflected under the relevant categories.

In addition, while material instances did not occur in this sample, the possibility exists in several countries that the classification of items as extraordinary, or the treatment of sales of significant businesses, may differ from IAS and US-GAAP. However, in such cases it is anticipated that the material adjustments would be between a local practice and revised IAS.[4]

Aside from the measurement aspects, several cases were found in which the companies would be required to provide additional disclosures under both IAS and US-GAAP.

3.2.G.   TAXATION

Taxation is frequently a large reconciling item in a Form 20-F reconciliation (Amir, Harris, and Venuti [1993]). However, it is useful to distinguish two categories within this one item. Current practice shows the pretax amounts of reconciling items with the tax impact incorporated into the taxation component of the reconciliation table. In addition, there may be differences in the application of the principles of calculating deferred taxes. Table 3 reflects all itemized adjustments as after tax so as to clearly differentiate the adjustments that relate to the taxation principles themselves.

US-GAAP for taxation has gone through a period of controversial change with the introduction of SFAS 96, its delayed application, and then subsequent replacement by SFAS 109. The new standard introduced several significant changes, including a change to a balance sheet approach for evaluating temporary (timing) differences.

---

4 The treatment under IAS is summarized in Appendix A.

IAS 12, which covers income taxes, is currently under revision and the final approach that will be taken remains an open question. Hence, the potential exists for a significant difference to remain between IAS and US-GAAP in this area.

In the sample, the most common area of measurement difference related to the recognition of deferred tax assets. Historically, in the US and currently under IAS and most country practices, conservatism has dictated a reluctance to recognize deferred tax assets unless the recovery of the tax is virtually assured. SFAS 109 requires recognition of all deferred tax assets, although these may be offset by a valuation allowance to reflect the uncertainty of realization. Consequently, one of the differences found, but not necessarily quantified, is unrecognized deferred tax assets, which arise primarily from net operating loss carryforwards. In 1993, the IASC allowed the partial and comprehensive methods of deferred tax recognition. Consequently, one of the sample companies used the partial method in applying IAS. This approach led to a significant under-accrual relative to US-GAAP.

Aside from the measurement differences, there was also a large difference between the disclosures provided by many of the companies and those disclosures required by US-GAAP. The proposed IAS [E49] will require enhanced disclosures so the difference likely will be narrowed once the new standard is adopted. The analysis also revealed a potentially interesting problem in applying US-GAAP to an institutional setting, which differs in a way that precludes useful information being generated. In Holderbank's case, the Swiss tax system, in conjunction with the multinational nature of the group, makes a reconciliation to a statutory tax rate a meaningless exercise.

Accounting for deferred taxes remains a controversial topic. As in other cases, part of the controversy revolves around the conflict between conservatism and matching. Different users and different countries' standard-setters place varying weights on the two concepts. Consequently, it is an area that is likely to remain as a potential difference.

3.2.H. POST-EMPLOYMENT BENEFITS

This area includes pensions, post-employment health benefits, and other post-employment costs that are covered by a number of different standards within US-GAAP. Historically, the US has emphasized private post-employment benefits more than other countries; nevertheless, this area has proven to be a major reconciling item for many non-US registrants (Amir, Harris, and Venuti [1993]). Revised IAS 19 considers accounting for pensions and in many respects is consistent with US-GAAP. One potential difference exists in the treatment of the assumed discount and asset return rates. US-GAAP requires adjustment for changes in market conditions, while IAS allows use of a long-run average rate. However, this potential difference did not seem to affect any of the sample companies. IAS 19 does not consider other post-employment benefits explicitly, although the standard does suggest that similar items be treated in an equivalent manner. The IASC is undertaking a major reevaluation of the whole area of accounting for post-employment benefits. Part of the question being addressed is the adequacy of IAS 19 for the complex institutional idiosyncrasies of different national systems. Consequently, IAS likely will evolve over the next few years in a manner that may move it further away from current US-GAAP.

Estimation of pension obligations based on the actuarial assumptions required by US-GAAP is an expensive process for a large multinational group. However, the sample companies had already used the US-GAAP basis for the major subsidiaries in applying either IAS or their own local standard. In three cases, the adjustment was made in order to comply with IAS. In another case, an adjustment was required to accrue for post-employment health care costs in conformity with SFAS 106, which did not have to be applied at the time of the annual report used for this analysis.

In sum, most of the material differences applied in moving to revised IAS, with little difference between revised IAS and US-GAAP. However, this was partially the result of the specific choices made by the set of companies in the sample. Furthermore, while the measurement differences were small, in the cases where no Form 20-F was provided there was a paucity of disclosure relative to that required by US-GAAP.

3.2.I. REVENUE RECOGNITION

In the sample of companies there was no material adjustment required. However, in a few cases there was a potential difference because the company used a completed contract method, which was allowed by IAS at the time. However, under revised IAS a percentage of completion approach must be applied. Hence, revenue recognition represents an example of a practice where revision of the standard has essentially eliminated the difference from US-GAAP.

3.2.J. SEGMENT REPORTING

IAS 14 has similar requirements to US-GAAP, although the latter has the additional requirement for disclosure of line-of-business data for capital expenditure and depreciation. The FASB and the IASC are working together to update their segment reporting requirements. While some differences have arisen in the development of their approaches, it is plausible that the two groups will end up with a standard that is consistent.

Despite the present consistency between IAS and US-GAAP, several companies did not supply segment data for operating income, in particular for geographic segments, despite their stated compliance with IAS. This case points to an issue discussed more fully in the conclusion, specifically, that there are cases in which companies indicate compliance or consistency with IAS, yet there are areas in which noncompliance occurs and the accounts do not comment on this.

Given the tension between investors' desire for more disaggregated data (Knutson [1993]) and companies' apparent concern for disclosing such data, it is hoped that the IASC and FASB can arrive at a consistent approach in their deliberations to avoid additional confusion in this sensitive area.

3.2.K. RELATED PARTY TRANSACTIONS

IAS 24 and US-GAAP require details of related party transactions. In many countries the institutional structures, concentration of share ownership, and nature of intercompany relationships may create circumstances that lead to transactions that fall under the umbrella of related party transactions. While management of the sample companies stated that all such transactions were disclosed, this area may present a difficulty for some potential non-US registrants. On the other hand, the Australian requirements were more extensive than those of IAS or US-GAAP.

Despite this note of caution, IAS requires disclosure of such transactions so that strict compliance with IAS should ensure that the SEC's concern for investor protection in this area is met adequately.

3.2.L. STATEMENT OF CASH FLOWS

A statement of cash flows is not required in several countries, although large international groups frequently supply some form of cash flow statement. IAS 7 and SFAS 95, the two standards dealing with cash flow statements, are similar. Hence, as the SEC has accepted compliance with IAS 7 as sufficient for a non-US registrant; where a sample company applied IAS 7 no required adjustments were indicated.

One issue that may merit some consideration is an apparent inconsistency between IAS 13 and IAS 7 (and therefore US-GAAP) in the classification of cash equivalents. IAS 7 uses a three-month maturity criterion, which is the same as US-GAAP. IAS 13 allows for a twelve-month period within the current liability classification. Anecdotal evidence suggests that the use of a three-month period for classification of cash equivalents is controversial, given the ready liquidity of many marketable securities with longer duration. Nevertheless, IAS and US-GAAP are consistent with respect to the cash flow statement definitions.

3.2.M. OTHER ITEMS

This subtopic covers a range of areas. The SEC requires a formalized management discussion and analysis [MD&A] section as part of the Form 20-F disclosures. While all our sample companies provided extensive discussion on issues that form part of the MD&A, most of them would have to formalize and extend these disclosures in a full registration process.

A second area of potential difference arises in the calculation of earnings per share. Currently, the FASB is reevaluating US-GAAP and IAS is silent on this issue. However, the IASC and FASB are working together on this project and it is possible, though far from certain, that they will agree on an equivalent standard going forward. Nevertheless, at present, non-US firms complying with IAS have no basis for calculating earnings per share other than local practice or US-GAAP.

In dynamic business environments, situations arise in which companies have to decide on appropriate accounting practice. As US-GAAP is more detailed and comprehensive than IAS, it is likely that in many of these situations US-GAAP will exist but neither IAS nor local practice will be defined. In several instances, the companies in the sample based their accounting practices on US-GAAP. Hence, US-GAAP has evidently proven to be a useful source for developing accounting practice.

3.3. SUMMARY

While differences remain between revised IAS and US-GAAP, the paucity of the specific measurement differences was surprising. Where material items did exist, they were largely either the result of the concession in IAS not to require retroactive adjustment for adoption of the requirements in the revised standards or of the incomplete development or revision of an IAS. On the other hand, there were more differences in the extent of disclosures, although even in this area the reasons were the same. That is, where IAS has gone through an extensive review process, the disclosures were found to be quite detailed (see Appendix A).

TABLE 2
Summary of Adjustments by Accounting Practice and Company

The Atlas Copco Group

Accounting Policy	As Reported to Revised IAS	From Revised IAS to US-GAAP
A. Acquisitions, Business Combinations, and Consolidations	Old pooling no longer valid. Potential adjustment for negative goodwill amortization. Disclose cumulative effect of an accounting change.	Adjust old pooling to purchase accounting. Cumulative effect of an accounting change.
B. Foreign Currency Translation	— —	Possibly adjust policy for subsidiaries operating in a hyperinflationary economy.[1] Reverse deferred exchange differences on short-term anticipated transactions.
C. Shareholders' Equity	Reclassification.	— —
D. Property, Plant, and Equipment	Possibly some capital (finance) leases. Possibly some development costs to be capitalized.	Interest capitalization. Reverse old revaluations.
E. Investments	Additional disclosures.	Possibly write down some marketable securities to historical cost.
F. Discontinued Operations and Changes in Accounting Policies	Reclassification and disclosure.	Cumulative effect of accounting change.

TABLE 2   The Atlas Copco Group   23

The Atlas Copco Group (cont.)

Accounting Policy	As Reported to Revised IAS	From Revised IAS to US-GAAP
G. Taxation	Reclassification and disclosures.	Disclosures.
H. Post-Employment Benefits	Possibly different accrual. Additional disclosures. Reclassification.	Possibly different accrual. Additional disclosures.
I. Revenue Recognition	Adjust to percentage of completion.	— —
J. Segment Reporting	Additional geographical disclosures.	Additional disclosure of depreciation.
K. Related Party Transactions	— —	—
L. Statement of Cash Flows	Cash flow statement required.	—
M. Other Items	Additional disclosures.	—

1 This adjustment would no longer apply under the new rules adopted by the SEC in December 1994.

TABLE 2 *The Bayer Group*

TABLE 2
Summary of Adjustments by Accounting Practice and Company

Accounting Policy	The Bayer Group	
	As Reported to Revised IAS	From Revised IAS to US-GAAP
A. Acquisitions, Business Combinations, and Consolidations	Capitalize and amortize goodwill. Additional disclosures.	Adjust for retroactive write-off of goodwill.
B. Foreign Currency Translation	Use current rate for all assets and average rate for income statements. Use current rate for all transaction balances.	— — —
C. Shareholders' Equity	Adjust for tax-related items. Reclassify minority interest. Additional disclosure.	— — —
D. Property, Plant, and Equipment	Capitalize certain leases. Additional disclosure. Possibly capitalize development costs.	Capitalize borrowing costs.
E. Investments	Additional disclosures.	Additional disclosures. Adjust to portfolio basis of calculation of lower of cost and market value.
F. Discontinued Operations and Changes in Accounting Policies	Potential reclassification and disclosure.	Potential reclassification and disclosure.
G. Taxation	Additional disclosure.	Additional disclosures. Possible deferred tax asset from net operating loss carryforwards.

TABLE 2   *The Bayer Group*   **25**

The Bayer Group (cont.)

Accounting Policy	As Reported to Revised IAS	From Revised IAS to US-GAAP
H. Post-Employment Benefits	Consider future salaries and alternate interest rates. Additional disclosures.	Additional disclosures.
I. Revenue Recognition	Use percentage of completion (potential only).	— — —
J. Segment Reporting	Disclosure of identified assets.	Additional disclosure of depreciation.
K. Related Party Transactions	— — —	— — —
L. Statement of Cash Flows	Reclassify.	— — —
M. Other Items	Treat bond-discount as contra-liability.	Management discussion and analysis. Additional disclosure of earnings per share.

Table 2
Summary of Adjustments by Accounting Practice and Company

The Broken Hill Proprietary Company Group

Accounting Policy	As Reported to Revised IAS	From Revised IAS to U.S.-GAAP
A. Acquisitions, Business Combinations, and Consolidations	Use equity accounting in primary financial statements.	—
B. Foreign Currency Translation	—	—
C. Shareholders' Equity	Reclassifications. Exclude minority shareholders' interest. Treat loan to ESOP as contra-equity (possibly).	Treat loan to ESOP as contra-equity.
D. Property, Plant, and Equipment	—	Exclude revaluations. Retroactive adjustment for interest capitalization. Supplementary oil and gas disclosures.
E. Investments	—	Additional disclosures. Exclude revaluations of long-term investments .
F. Discontinued Operations and Changes in Accounting Policies	Reclassifications.	—
G. Taxation	Reclassifications.	Additional disclosures.
H. Post-Employment Benefits	Accrue on a present value basis. Additional disclosures.	Additional disclosures.

TABLE 2   The Broken Hill Proprietary Company Group   **27**

The Broken Hill Proprietary Company Group (cont.)

Accounting Policy	As Reported to Revised IAS	From Revised IAS to U.S.-GAAP
I. Revenue Recognition	— —	— —
J. Segment Reporting	— —	Additional disclosure of depreciation and capital expenditures.
K. Related Party Transactions	— —	— —
L. Statement of Cash Flows	— —	— —
M. Other Items	— —	— —

TABLE 2   *The Cap Gemini Sogeti Group*

Table 2
Summary of Adjustments by Accounting Practice and Company

Accounting Policy	The Cap Gemini Sogeti Group	
	As Reported to Revised IAS	From Revised IAS to US-GAAP
A. Acquisitions, Business Combinations, and Consolidations	Exclude market share and transfer to goodwill. Adjust goodwill for deferred payments. Possibly reduce goodwill amortization period. Increased disclosure. Reclassify goodwill in associated companies.	Adjustment for market value of investment prior to increase in shareholding to the level of control.
B. Foreign Currency Translation	Additional disclosures.	— — —
C. Shareholders' Equity	— — —	Adjust for companies premium on bonds. Compensation expense on stock options. Additional disclosures.
D. Property, Plant, and Equipment	Expense internally generated software. Additional disclosure of lease payments.	— — —
E. Investments	— — —	Set up contra-equity account for difference between cost and market value of long-term investment. Additional disclosures.

TABLE 2   The Cap Gemini Sogeti Group

The Cap Gemini Sogeti Group (cont).

Accounting Policy	As Reported to Revised IAS	From Revised IAS to US-GAAP
F. Discontinued Operations and Changes in Accounting Policies	— —	— —
G. Taxation	— —	Possibly additional deferred tax asset. Possibly additional disclosures.
H. Post-Employment Benefits	Additional disclosures.	Additional disclosures.
I. Revenue Recognition	Additional disclosures.	— —
J. Segment Reporting	Disclose operating income and assets by geographical segment.	— —
K. Related Party Transactions	— —	Possibly reverse gains on related party transactions.
L. Statement of Cash Flows	Disclosure of interest and tax separately.	— —
M. Other Items	— —	Reverse in substance defeasance. Management discussion and analysis.

Table 2
Summary of Adjustments by Accounting Practice and Company

The Fletcher Challenge Group

Accounting Policy	As Reported to Revised IAS	From Revised IAS to US-GAAP
A. Acquisitions, Business Combinations, and Consolidations	— —	Adjustment for net operating losses in acquired companies.
B. Foreign Currency Translation	Apply average rates to income and cash flow statements. Adjust treatment of hedges of anticipated transactions.	— —
C. Shareholders' Equity	Reclassification.	Reclassification. Adjust for proposed dividend.
D. Property, Plant, and Equipment	Disclosure detail.	— —
E. Investments	— —	— —
F. Discontinued Operations and Changes in Accounting Policies	— —	Reflect cumulative effect of change in accounting principle.
G. Taxation	— —	Additional disclosures.
H. Post-Employment Benefits	— —	— —
I. Revenue recognition	— —	— —
J. Segment Reporting	— —	Additional disclosure of depreciation and capital expenditures.

TABLE 2   *The Fletcher Challenge Group*   31

The Fletcher Challenge Group (cont.)

Accounting Policy	As Reported to Revised IAS			From Revised IAS to US-GAAP		
K. Related Party Transactions	—	—		—	—	
L. Statement of Cash Flows	—	—		—	—	
M. Other Items	—	—		—	—	

TABLE 2
Summary of Adjustments by Accounting Practice and Company

	The Holderbank Group	
Accounting Policy	As Reported to Revised IAS	From Revised IAS to US-GAAP
A. Acquisitions, Business Combinations, and Consolidations	— —	Retroactive application of goodwill capitalization. Unconsolidate one company.
B. Foreign Currency Translation	— —	Possible adjustment for companies operating in hyperinflationary economies.[1]
C. Shareholders' Equity	Reclassification of minority shareholders' interest.	— —
D. Property, Plant, and Equipment	— —	— —
E. Investments	Limited reclassification.	Mark down marketable securities to historical cost.
F. Discontinued Operations and Changes in Accounting Policy	— —	Retroactive adjustment for changes in accounting policy.
G. Taxation	— —	Additional disclosures. Use of comprehensive method.
H. Post-Employment Benefits	— —	Change in accrual as a result of adjusted actuarial assumptions. Additional disclosures.
I. Revenue Recognition	— —	— —

TABLE 2   *The Holderbank Group*

33

The Holderbank Group (cont.)

	Accounting Policy	As Reported to Revised IAS	From Revised IAS to US-GAAP
J.	Segment Reporting	Geographical disclosures (provided in 1993).	Depreciation disclosure for line of business.
K.	Related Party Transactions	— —	Possibly more details.
L.	Statement of Cash Flows	Reclassify cash equivalents.	— — —
M.	Other Items	Reclassification.	Additional management discussion and analysis disclosures.

---

1 This adjustment may no longer apply under the new rules adopted by the SEC in December 1994.

TABLE 2
Summary of Adjustments by Accounting Practice and Company

Accounting Policy	The Olivetti Group	
	As Reported to Revised IAS	From Revised IAS to US-GAAP
A. Acquisitions, Business Combinations, and Consolidations	Capitalize and amortize goodwill. Consolidate all subsidiaries.	Adjust for retroactive write-off of goodwill.
B. Foreign Currency Translation	— —	Possibly adjust method for subsidiaries operating in a hyperinflationary economy.[1] Adjust deferral of exchange loss included in inventory.
C. Shareholders' Equity	— —	Compensation expense for certain options. Write off issuance costs. Adjust for implied value in detachable warrants in bonds.
D. Property, Plant, and Equipment	— —	Exclude revaluations. Additional disclosures.
E. Investments	— —	Change basis of portfolio classification for lower of cost and market rules.
F. Discontinued Operations and Changes in Accounting Policies	— —	— —
G. Taxation	Charge tax on shareholders' equity to income. Additional disclosures.	Additional disclosures. Possible additional accrual.

TABLE 2   *The Olivetti Group*   **35**

The Olivetti Group (cont.)

Accounting Policy	As Reported to Revised IAS	From Revised IAS to US-GAAP
H. Post-Employment Benefits	Additional disclosures. Possible adjustment to accrual.	Additional disclosures. Possible adjustment to accrual.
I. Revenue Recognition	Use percentage of completion method.	— — —
J. Segment Reporting	Disclose operating income for geographic segments.	— — —
K. Related Party Transactions	— — —	Additional disclosures.
L. Statement of Cash Flows	Prepare cash flow statement.	— — —
M. Other Items	— — —	Earnings per share. Management discussion and analysis.

1   This adjustment may no longer apply under the new rules adopted by the SEC in December 1994.

TABLE 2   *The Valeo Group*

TABLE 2
Summary of Adjustments by Accounting Practice and Company

Accounting Policy	The Valeo Group	
	As Reported to Revised IAS	From Revised IAS to US-GAAP
A. Acquisitions, Business Combinations, and Consolidations	Reduce maximum amortization period for goodwill to 20 years.	— —
B. Foreign Currency Translation	Amortize difference between spot and hedge rate over life of hedge contract.	Possibly adjust method for entities operating in a hyperinflationary environment.[1]
C. Shareholders' Equity	— —	Reflect discount on issue of shares to employees as compensation expense (currently immaterial).
D. Property, Plant, and Equipment	Possibly capitalize certain development costs.	— —
E. Investments	— —	— —
F. Discontinued Operations and Changes in Accounting Policies	Probable reclassification. Possible additional disclosure.	Additional disclosures.
G. Taxation	— —	Recognize deferred tax assets. Additional disclosures.
H. Post-Employment Benefits	— —	Additional disclosures.
I. Revenue Recognition	— —	— —
J. Segment Reporting	Operating income disclosures.	Depreciation disclosure for line of business.

TABLE 2   The Valeo Group   **37**

The Valeo Group (cont.)

Accounting Policy	As Reported to Revised IAS	From Revised IAS to US-GAAP
K. Related Party Transactions	— — —	— — —
L. Statement of Cash Flows	Reclassifications. Additional disclosures.	— — —
M. Other Items	— —	Management discussion and analysis. Disclosures on earnings per share.

1 This adjustment may no longer apply under the new rules adopted by the SEC in December 1994.

TABLE 3
Impact of Adjustments on Shareholders' Equity

The Atlas Copco Group
December 31, 1992

| | Increase/(Decrease) | | |
Area Covered	As Reported to Revised IAS (millions)	Revised IAS to US-GAAP* (millions)	Comments
Acquisitions, Business Combinations, and Consolidations	SEK 0.0	SEK 472.0	Retroactive adjustment for treatment of acquisition as a purchase.
Foreign Currency Translation	0.0	0.0	
Shareholders' Equity:			
Dividends	0.0	0.0	
Minority interest	0.0	0.0	
Property, Plant, and Equipment:			
Interest capitalization	0.0	76.0	Retroactive adjustment.
Revaluation	0.0	(31.0)	Revaluation of fixed assets is not permitted.
Investments	0.0	0.0	
Discontinued Operations and Changes in Accounting Policies	0.0	0.0	

The Atlas Copco Group (cont.)

Area Covered	As Reported to Revised IAS	Revised IAS to US-GAAP*	Comments
	(millions)	(millions)	
Taxation (1)	0.0	0.0	
Post-Employment Benefits(2)	0.0	(100.0)	Accrual of post-employment health care benefits.
Other	0.0	0.0	
Net Adjustment to Shareholders' Equity	SEK 0.0	SEK 417.0	
Shareholders' Equity as Reported at December 31, 1992	SEK 7,295.0	SEK 7,295.0	

SEK 1= 0.1425 US$ at December 31, 1992

* United States Generally Accepted Accounting Principles as required for Foreign Private Issuers filing Form 20-F

(1) The tax effects of all other adjustments are reflected in the other adjustment amounts.

(2) Under US-GAAP, companies were only required to adopt SFAS 106 in 1993. Atlas Copco adopted SFAS 106 in 1993. Other potential adjustments for Swedish and German subsidiaries were not quantified.

This table should be read in conjunction with the information in Chapter 3 and Appendix B.

TABLE 3
Impact of Adjustments on Shareholders' Equity

The Bayer Group
December 31, 1993

Area Covered	Increase/(Decrease)		Comments
	As Reported to Revised IAS	Revised IAS to US-GAAP*	
	(millions)	(millions)	
Acquisitions, Business Combinations, and Consolidations	DM 0.0	DM 1,116.7	Retroactive adjustment for previous write-offs of goodwill.
Foreign Currency Translation			
Unrealized gains	12.0	0.0	Recognition of unrealized foreign currency gains.
Translation	(429.0)	0.0	Use of current rate method.
Shareholders' Equity:			
Dividends	.0	0.0	Minority interest presented separately from shareholders' equity.
Minority interest	(479.0)	0.0	Reversal of the "Special item with an equity component" (net of
Other	78.0	0.0	applicable deferred taxes) and reversal of tax write-downs.
Property, Plant, and Equipment:			
Interest capitalization	0.0	0.0	
Revaluation	0.0	0.0	
Development costs	0.0	0.0	
Investments	0.0	0.0	

The Bayer Group (cont.)

Area Covered	As Reported to Revised IAS (millions)	Revised IAS to US-GAAP* (millions)	Comments
Discontinued Operations and Changes in Accounting Policies	0.0	0.0	
Taxation (1)	0.0	NQ	Possible deferred tax asset from operating loss carryforwards.
Post-Employment Benefits	(16.0)	0.0	Additional accrual allocated over the remaining service life.
Other	21.0	0.0	Reversal of future maintenance costs.
Net Adjustment to Shareholders' Equity	DM　(813.0)	DM　1,116.7	
Shareholders' Equity as Reported at December 31, 1993	DM　18,160.0	DM　18,160.0	

DM 1= 0.579 US$ at December 31, 1993

* United States Generally Accepted Accounting Principles as required for Foreign Private Issuers filing Form 20-F

NQ Potential difference has not been quantified

(1) The tax effects of all other adjustments are reflected in the other adjustment amounts.

This table should be read in conjunction with the information in Chapter 3 and Appendix B.

TABLE 3
Impact of Adjustments on Shareholders' Equity

The Broken Hill Proprietary Company Group
May 31, 1993

Area Covered	Increase/(Decrease)		Comments
	As Reported to Revised IAS (millions)	Revised IAS to US-GAAP* (millions)	
Acquisitions, Business Combinations, and Consolidations	A$ 203.0	A$ 0.0	Application of equity method.
Foreign Currency Translation	0.0	0.0	
Shareholders' Equity:			
Dividends	0.0	0.0	
Minority interest	0.0	0.0	
Other	0.0	(796.0)	Loans made to employees for the purchase of shares of the Company are classified as a contra-equity account.
Property, Plant, and Equipment:			
Interest capitalization	0.0	15.0	Retroactive adjustment.
Revaluation	0.0	(268.0)	Reverse revaluation of fixed assets.
Other	0.0	(83.0)	Old application of "successful efforts" method.
Investments	0.0	(24.0)	Reverse upward revaluation of investments.
Discontinued Operations and Changes in Accounting Policies	0.0	0.0	

The Broken Hill Proprietary Company Group (cont.)

Area Covered	As Reported to Revised IAS	Revised IAS to US-GAAP*	Comments
	(millions)	(millions)	
Taxation (1)	0.0	0.0	
Post-Employment Benefits	71.0	0.0	Accrual based approach for pension accounting.
Other	0.0	0.0	
Net Adjustment to Shareholders' Equity	A$ 274.0	A$ (1,156.0)	
Shareholders' Equity as Reported at May 31, 1993	A$ 8,867.0	A$ 8,867.0	

Australian 1$ = 0.6862 US$ at May 31, 1993
* United States Generally Accepted Accounting Principles as required for Foreign Private Issuers filing Form 20-F
(1) The tax effects of all other adjustments are reflected in the other adjustment amounts.
This table should be read in conjunction with the information in Chapter 3 and Appendix B.

TABLE 3
Impact of Adjustments on Shareholders' Equity

The Cap Gemini Sogeti Group
December 31, 1992

Area Covered	Increase/(Decrease)		Comments
	As Reported to Revised IAS	Revised IAS to US-GAAP*	
	(millions)	(millions)	
Acquisitions, Business Combinations, and Consolidations			
Purchase accounting	FF (78.0)	FF 0.0	Adjustment for deferred payment at acquisition.
	0.0	(200.0)	Retroactively apply purchase accounting for change from equity accounting.
Intangible asset classification	0.0	(85.0)	Retroactive adjustment for reclassification of "market share" intangible asset to goodwill.
Amortization of intangibles	(400.0)	0.0	Retroactive adjustment to 20-year amortization period for goodwill, assumed write-off under revised IAS.
Foreign Currency Translation	0.0	0.0	
Shareholders' Equity:			
Dividends	0.0	0.0	
Minority interest	0.0	0.0	
Property, Plant, and Equipment:			
Interest capitalization	0.0	0.0	
Revaluation	0.0	0.0	
Other	(12.0)	0.0	The costs of internally developed software are expensed.
Investments	0.0	(153.0)	Reduce investment to market value.

The Cap Gemini Sogeti Group (cont.)

Area Covered	As Reported to Revised IAS (millions)	Revised IAS to US-GAAP* (millions)	Comments
Discontinued Operations and Changes in Accounting Policies	0.0	0.0	
Taxation (1)	0.0	NQ	Deferred tax assets have not been recognized for operating loss carryforwards.
Post-Employment Benefits	0.0	0.0	
Other	0.0	(20.0)	Reversal of in-substance defeasance.
Net Adjustment to Shareholders' Equity	FF (490.0)	FF (458.0)	
Shareholders' Equity as Reported at December 31, 1992	FF 5,171.5	FF 5,171.5	

1 FF = 0.182 US$ at December 31, 1992

* United States Generally Accepted Accounting Principles as required for Foreign Private Issuers filing Form 20-F

NQ Potential difference has not been quantified

(1) The tax effects of all other adjustments are reflected in the other adjustment amounts.

This table should be read in conjunction with the information in Chapter 3 and Appendix B.

TABLE 3
Impact of Adjustments on Shareholders' Equity

	The Fletcher Challenge Group June 30, 1993		
	Increase/(Decrease)		
Area Covered	As Reported to Revised IAS (millions)	Revised IAS to US-GAAP* (millions)	Comments
Acquisitions, Business Combinations, and Consolidations	NZ$ 0.0	NZ$ (59.7)	A deferred tax asset would be recognized as part of the purchase price allocation related to the value of unutilized tax loss carryforwards.
Foreign Currency Translation	0.0	0.0	
Shareholders' Equity: Dividends	0.0	86.1	Add back proposed dividends.
Minority interest	0.0	0.0	
Property, Plant, and Equipment: Interest capitalization	0.0	0.0	
Revaluation	0.0	0.0	
Investments	0.0	0.0	
Discontinued Operations and Changes in Accounting Policies	0.0	0.0	

The Fletcher Challenge Group (cont.)

Area Covered	As Reported to Revised IAS	Revised IAS to US-GAAP*	Comments
	(millions)	(millions)	
Taxation (1)	0.0	0.0	
Post-Employment Benefits	0.0	0.0	
Other	0.0	0.0	
Net Adjustment to Shareholders' Equity	NZ$ 0.0	NZ$ 26.4	
Shareholders' Equity as Reported at June 30, 1993	NZ$ 3,891.9	NZ$ 3,891.9	

1 NZ$ = 0.5382 US$ at June 30, 1993
* United States Generally Accepted Accounting Principles as required for Foreign Private Issuers filing Form 20-F
(1) The tax effects of all other adjustments are reflected in the other adjustment amounts.
This table should be read in conjunction with the information in Chapter 3 and Appendix B.

Table 3 Impact of Adjustments on Shareholders' Equity: The Holderbank Group

TABLE 3
Impact of Adjustments on Shareholders' Equity

The Holderbank Group
December 31, 1992

Area Covered	Increase/(Decrease)		Comments
	As Reported to Revised IAS	Revised IAS to US-GAAP*	
	(millions)	(millions)	
Acquisitions, Business Combinations, and Consolidations	SFr 0.0	SFr 164.0	Retroactive adjustment to reflect goodwill net of amortization.
Foreign Currency Translation	0.0	NQ	Use of Swiss Franc as functional currency for subsidiaries in hyperinflationary economies has not been quantified.
Shareholders' Equity:			
Dividends	0.0	0.0	
Minority interest	0.0	0.0	
Property, Plant, and Equipment:			
Interest capitalization	0.0	0.0	
Revaluation	0.0	0.0	
Investments	0.0	0.0	
Discontinued Operations and Changes in Accounting Policies	0.0	0.0	

The Holderbank Group (cont.)

Area Covered	As Reported to Revised IAS (millions)	Revised IAS to US-GAAP* (millions)	Comments
Taxation (1)	0.0	(225.0)	Use of comprehensive versus partial method, net of minority interest.
Post-Employment Benefits	(20.0)	0.0	Additional accrual required for German subsidiaries made in 1993.
Other	0.0	0.0	
Net Adjustment to Shareholders' Equity	SFr (20.0)	SFr (61.0)	
Shareholders' Equity as Reported at December 31, 1992	SFr 3,005.0	SFr 3,005.0	

SFr 1= 0.68 US$ at December 31, 1992

* United States Generally Accepted Accounting Principles as required for Foreign Private Issuers filing Form 20-F

NQ Potential difference has not been quantified

(1) The tax effects of all other adjustments are reflected in the other adjustment amounts.

This table should be read in conjunction with the information in Chapter 3 and Appendix B.

TABLE 3
Impact of Adjustments on Shareholders' Equity

The Olivetti Group
December 31, 1992

Area Covered	Increase/(Decrease)		Comments
	As Reported to Revised IAS (millions)	Revised IAS to US-GAAP* (millions)	
Acquisitions, Business Combinations, and Consolidations	Lira 0.0	Lira 100.0	Retroactive adjustment for write-off of goodwill.
Foreign Currency Translation	0.0	(6.0)	Exchange differences resulting from a significant devaluation of the Lira against other currencies were treated as part of purchase cost rather than as translation losses. Other potential differences arising from the translation of subsidiaries in hyperinflationary economies were not quantified.
Shareholders' Equity:			
Dividends	0.0	0.0	
Minority interest	0.0	0.0	
Capital issuance costs	0.0	(3.0)	Costs of issuing capital are deferred and amortized by Olivetti but would be written off against equity.
Stock options and warrants	0.0	180.0	Balance of imputed value from bonds issued with detachable warrants.
Property, Plant, and Equipment:			
Interest capitalization	0.0	0.0	
Revaluation	0.0	(240.0)	Revaluations required or permitted under Italian tax law.
Investments	0.0	0.0	
Discontinued Operations and Changes in Accounting Policies	0.0	0.0	

Table 3   Impact of Adjustments on Shareholders' Equity: The Olivetti Group

The Olivetti Group (cont.)

Area Covered	As Reported to Revised IAS	Revised IAS to US-GAAP*	Comments
	(millions)	(millions)	
Taxation (1)	4.0	NQ	Quantification of differences between tax and book bases of all assets and liabilities not considered feasible for purposes of this study. Large net operating loss carryforwards exist.
Post-Employment Benefits	0.0	0.0	Estimate based on 1989 amounts, no precise amounts quantified.
Revenue Recognition	0.0	0.0	Revenue earned under long-term contracts is recognized using a milestone method (rather than percentage of completion). No significant difference is expected.
Other	0.0	0.0	
Net Adjustment to Shareholders' Equity	Lira 4.0	Lira 31.0	
Shareholders' Equity as Reported at December 31, 1992	Lira 2,361.2	Lira 2,361.2	

Italian Lira 1000 = 0.68 US$ at December 31, 1992
* United States Generally Accepted Accounting Principles as required for Foreign Private Issuers filing Form 20-F
NQ Potential difference has not been quantified
(1) The tax effects of all other adjustments are reflected in the other adjustment amounts.
This table should be read in conjunction with the information in Chapter 3 and Appendix B.

TABLE 3
Impact of Adjustments on Shareholders' Equity

Area Covered	The Valeo Group December 31, 1992		Comments
	Increase/(Decrease)		
	As Reported to Revised IAS (millions)	Revised IAS to US-GAAP* (millions)	
Acquisitions, Business Combinations, and Consolidations	FF 0.0	FF 0.0	Information was not available to make an assessment of any retroactive adjustment that may be necessary under US-GAAP.
Foreign Currency Translation	0.0	NQ	The effect of using the US dollar as the functional currency for an associated company in a hyperinflationary economy has not been quantified.
Shareholders' Equity:			
Dividends	0.0	0.0	
Minority interest	0.0	0.0	
Employee stock options	0.0	(8.0)	Estimated compensation expense for options issued below market value.
Property, Plant, and Equipment:			
Interest capitalization	0.0	0.0	
Revaluation	0.0	0.0	
Investments	0.0	0.0	
Discontinued Operations and Changes in Accounting Policies	0.0	0.0	

The Valeo Group (cont.)

Area Covered	As Reported to Revised IAS	Revised IAS to US-GAAP*	Comments
	(millions)	(millions)	
Taxation (1)	0.0	422.0	Accrual of deferred tax assets as shown in the notes to the 1992 annual report.
Post-Employment Benefits	0.0	0.0	
Other	0.0	0.0	
Net Adjustment to Shareholders' Equity	FF 0.0	FF 414.0	
Shareholders' Equity as Reported at December 31, 1992	FF 7,213.0	FF 7,213.0	

1 FF= 0.182 US$ at December 31, 1992
* United States Generally Accepted Accounting Principles as required for Foreign Private Issuers filing Form 20-F
NQ Potential difference has not been quantified
(1) The tax effects of all other adjustments are reflected in the other adjustment amounts.
This table should be read in conjunction with the information in Chapter 3 and Appendix B.

4

CONCLUSION

At the outset of this project, the set of reconciliations from revised IAS to US-GAAP was expected to be smaller than the perceived flexibility of IAS would imply. Nevertheless, outside of the retroactive adjustments, the paucity of reconciling items was surprising. The caveats to the findings cannot be dismissed given the sample selection process and its size, and given the lack of a detailed audit of the data. But it is apparent from this analysis that opponents of IAS who argue that adoption of IAS will hurt investors by lowering the standard of financial reporting need to reevaluate that position.

The natural questions that evolve from the analysis are: how could adoption of IAS for non-US registrants be implemented, what are the concerns or pitfalls that follow, and how can the various players reduce these potential problems? These questions are considered in the context of the analysis in order to stimulate a rational discussion of the issues.

4.1 IMPLEMENTING IAS FOR NON-US REGISTRANTS

The SEC is correctly concerned with protecting the rights of US investors. In fulfilling this function, not only does the SEC have the final say over the establishment of US-GAAP but, through the Division of Corporation Finance, it also evaluates the information registrants provide. If the SEC accepted IAS for non-US registrants, the SEC would still be able to ensure that investors are protected by ensuring, via their review process, that the financial data conform with IAS in an acceptable manner. They would also rely on the auditors to perform their role in ensuring that the information is a fair representation of the financial condition and operating results of the firm.

The trend of US investors moving their funds into non-US investments is well documented (Cochrane [1994]). This trend is occurring despite the lack of US-GAAP reconciliations and is not limited to the large institutions. Furthermore, the volume of activity in Level I American Depositary Receipts (Velli [1994]) suggests that non-US firms are accessing the capital of

US investors in the US, while being exempt from the SEC's formal registration procedures. Consequently, we conjecture that by allowing a set of measurement rules which are not labelled US-GAAP, yet are developed from the investors' perspective, and which enable companies to report one set of financial measures, the SEC will enhance the availability of information to US investors and bring more companies into the US regulatory fold. To the extent this occurs, there will be enhanced disclosure on an array of issues (incorporating the non-reconciliation requirements of Form 20-F) and regulatory oversight. If the SEC believes that a company is hurting investors by obfuscating the information despite apparent compliance with IAS, then it has the right to impose its regulatory control if the company is registered.

The most potent arguments against this suggestion are the concern over the implications for US registrants and the potential lack of comparability for investors. While clearly valid, these concerns are probably overstated. Accounting systems evolve in the context of a broad set of institutional arrangements. As argued in Harris [1993], forcing a set of rules developed in one environment onto a company operating in a fundamentally different institutional setting does not necessarily result in more value-relevant information. Hence, it is conceivable that there is a set of accounting rules that is relevant for US companies but that may not be equally relevant for Swiss or German companies. On the other hand, situations may arise in which there may be a conflict in which the FASB and IASC differ and US, or non-US, companies feel prejudiced. This situation does not really differ from what is occurring now. The FASB has worked in a number of ways to develop its standards in consideration of, and sometimes in cooperation with, other national standard setters and the IASC. Acceptance of IAS will only serve to enhance this cooperative spirit. But it is naive to believe that, currently, US companies are not competing for funds with non-US companies which are complying with a different set of accounting standards.

While some of the above comments also apply to the comparability concern, it is also worthwhile to note that in many of the areas in which IAS may differ from US-GAAP there are differences in the application of the accounting standards among US companies. One needs to look no further than the opportunities that exist in the accounting treatment of business combinations to appreciate this point.

One final point that needs to be made arises from the concern that IAS is not comprehensive enough and that, once the IASC has developed more standards, IAS may be acceptable. This notion seems to be consistent with the approach being taken by the International Organization of Securities Commissions [IOSCO], which has deemed some IAS as acceptable, but has also identified issues which need to be addressed before they endorse IAS (*IASC Insight*, September 1994). At some level, this process is appropriate but it also may never end. The FASB and other accounting standard setters continue to expend great effort and resources in developing standards. At the very least this process suggests that accounting standards evolve over time. Consequently, we must presume that no set of standards will ever be complete. Yet, the SEC and other members of IOSCO work within such an environment and allow GAAP to evolve while imposing their own regulations from time to time. IAS could be treated the same way. The analysis in this monograph suggests that revised IAS provides a set of standards that is quite comprehensive, and concerns over nuances may be counterproductive to the stated aims of IOSCO members.

4.2 CHALLENGES FOR THE IASC

While our analysis has demonstrated that IAS are more comprehensive and useful than some observers may have perceived, the IASC has some serious challenges ahead if it wants to take its place as a significant standard setter in the global equity markets.

IASC Board members provide their services on a voluntary basis and are appointed by various national or international organizations. As such, the quality of the board members and the amount of effort each is willing to invest in the process can be of high variance. In addition, the technical support in the IASC Secretariat is constrained by its resources which are paltry in comparison with the resources available to the FASB and some other standard setters. As IAS become more widely accepted, Board appointments and the standard setting process itself can be expected to become increasingly politicized. This process creates both potential opportunities and dangers. For example, the IASC should try to find a way to include member country standard setters in the process, but only if that does not cause the process to become bogged down in endless debate. Current rules make this approach difficult in many cases, but that does not mean it is impossible.

In addition, the IASC should seriously reevaluate some of its processes, building on its success to date while trying to avoid the pitfalls that naturally lie ahead. For example, the IASC must conclude its financial instruments project as soon as possible. This project was undertaken jointly with the Canadian Institute and has become mired in debate. Not only is the investment community obviously concerned about the accounting problems in the financial instruments area, but the project serves as a test of how the IASC will achieve a balance between concept and detailed regulation in developing a standard for complex issues.

Resolution of such issues may be facilitated if the IASC makes its process more public. Having IASC Board meetings open to the public will help to ensure that Board members represent the views of their constituents and carefully reason their arguments.[1]

---

1 I am grateful to Jim Leisenring of the FASB for making this suggestion to me.

4.3 CHALLENGES FOR THE ACCOUNTING REGULATORS

References have already been made to issues affecting the IASC and SEC. Analysis reveals that each country has idiosyncratic accounting principles which create a series of differences among financial reporting systems that seem difficult to understand. As already stated, there may be valid reasons for different countries requiring different accounting information to reflect their own institutional environment. However, it should be no surprise that many accounting rules evolve as the outcome of a consensus building process among the rule-makers. So, for example, an FASB standard, while developed within the bounds of a conceptual framework, must reflect the practices which are acceptable to a majority (currently five out of seven), but not necessarily all, of the board members. A similar process occurs in the IASC and in many other countries. What is difficult to comprehend, and where a challenge exists for several countries' regulators, as well as academic researchers, is how countries with apparently similar capital market and regulatory institutions can arrive at such different conclusions on many issues. Further, and perhaps more importantly, what is the economic justification to continue with the approach of having such independent systems?

An explicit example will illustrate this point. BHP presents its primary financial statements in conformity with Australian accounting standards. As such, it is precluded from applying equity accounting in its consolidated balance sheet and income statements. While there are pros and cons to the application of equity accounting, it seems to be hard to argue that the institutional arrangements in Australia are so different from those in Canada, New Zealand, and the UK, so as to warrant the difference in treatment. It is conjectured that each nation's standard setters would be well served to reconsider their own process in the light of the evolution of global capital markets and the existence of IAS. Hopefully, the evidence presented here might help to facilitate some reevaluation of these processes in the context of the two benchmarks of IAS and US-GAAP.

4.4 CHALLENGES FOR THE AUDITING PROFESSION

If IAS serve as a useful benchmark for firms listing on international capital markets, then the auditing profession will face new challenges. As observed in Chapter 1, and as so clearly articulated in the recent report to the Public Oversight Board [1994], the auditing profession has seemed to have moved (or been pushed) in the direction of seeking "bright lines" and then using these rules, rather than professional judgment and economic reasoning, to evaluate appropriate accounting practice.[2] IAS do not provide narrowly

---

2 Acher [1995] expresses a similar view of the profession's approach in the UK.

defined rules in many cases, and IAS are unlikely to move in that direction. Thus, the auditing profession will have to make judgments and focus on the economic substance of transactions rather than the narrow articulation of a set of rules. The profession will also have to be more consistent in its enforcement of compliance with IAS. This judgmental approach need not be viewed as bad news for investors. No group of standard setters which follows a system of public due process can ever hope to write a set of sufficiently detailed rules to cover the complexity and dynamic nature of the global business environment. Investors will have to rely on directors, managers, and auditors to provide the information with integrity, albeit within the framework of a set of accounting standards. If this system works, then the information will be economically relevant. Compliance with a rigid set of narrowly defined rules does not guarantee economic relevance of the resulting data.

The case studies presented in this monograph suggest that International Accounting Standards, as recently revised, warrant serious consideration as a viable framework of accounting standards, at least for those companies seeking capital in the major international capital markets. It remains to be seen whether the political processes involved will allow the IAS to succeed. But our hope is that the parties involved will now be able to debate these issues with some empirical evidence in hand.

APPENDIX A
Summary of International Accounting Standards and Additional Requirements Under Item 18 of Form 20-F as of October 31, 1994[1]

Stan-dard No.	Area Covered	Measurement Principles	Disclosure Requirements
1	Disclosure of Accounting Policies	Not applicable but defines fundamental assumptions and policies: going concern, consistency, matching (accrual), prudence, substance over form, materiality.	All significant accounting policies disclosed in one place. Disclosure does not rectify wrong or inappropriate treatment in the financial statements. Corresponding figures for preceding period. Material changes in accounting policies must be disclosed and quantified.
2	Inventories (Revised 1993)	Lower of cost and net realizable value (as defined). Costs should include costs of purchase, conversion, and other related costs. Benchmark: First in, first out or weighted average. Allowed Alternative: Last in, first out.	Measurement approach and cost formula used. Carrying amount in total and by appropriate classification. Carrying amount at net realizable value. Amount and circumstances leading to reversal of write-down. Carrying amount pledged as security. When LIFO is used, the equivalent amount under the benchmark or current cost. Cost of inventories used or classified operating costs recognized as an expense. Disclose information regarding general and administrative costs allocated to inventory. If LIFO method is used, additional disclosure is required.

Stan-dard No.	Area Covered	Measurement Principles	Disclosure Requirements
3	Superseded	— — —	— — —
4	Depreciation Accounting (mostly superseded)	See IAS 16—essentially same principles apply to intangible assets.	As for measurement principles.
5	Information to be disclosed in financial statements	Not applicable. Redeemable preferred shares whose redemption is outside the control of the issue should not be included in shareholders' equity.	Detailed and general disclosure items defined, including all material information that is necessary to make the financial statements clear and understandable. Commitments for capital expenditure. First-time, non-US registrants must provide a reconciliation of financial statements and selected financial data for the two most recently completed fiscal years (and any interim periods). Three years of audited income and cash flow statements and five years of selected income and balance sheet data are required. Earnings per share information must be calculated and disclosed. Disclose information regarding financial instruments with off-balance sheet risk, with concentrations of credit risk and those used as hedges.

Stan-dard No.	Area Covered	Measurement Principles	Disclosure Requirements
			When restricted net assets of consolidated subsidiaries exceed 25% (now 30%) of consolidated net assets, provide condensed financial information for the parent. Various other supplemental schedules are required, although recent SEC rulings have eliminated many of these.
			Effects of adopting accounting standards issued but not yet effective must be disclosed.
			Disclose separately other assets in excess of 5% of total assets and explain significant additions or deletions. Also disclose the policy for deferral and amortization of significant deferred changes.
			Disclose amounts and terms of significant unused lines of credit.
			Disclose cash compensating balances.
			Disclose selling, general, and administrative expenses separately.
			Disclose various information regarding environmental liabilities.
			Disclose separately other liabilities in excess of 5% of total liabilities.
6	Superseded	— — — —	— — —

Standard No.	Area Covered	Measurement Principles	Disclosure Requirements
7	Cash Flow Statements (Revised 1992)	Defines cash and cash equivalents. Allows netting of certain cash flows under restricted circumstances. Foreign currency cash flows translated at exchange rate when cash flows occurred.	Cash flow statement presented under either direct or indirect method. Must distinguish cash flows from operating, investing, and financing activities. Cash flows from interest, dividends, and taxes must be disclosed separately. Detailed disclosures on acquisitions and disposals of subsidiaries and other business units. Components of cash and cash equivalents. Cash held but not available for use. Additional disclosures encouraged include: Borrowing facilities available. Cash flows representing increases in operating capacity. Cash flows by segment.
8	Net Profit or Loss for the Period, Fundamental Errors and Changes in Accounting Policies (Revised 1993)	Extraordinary items defined as arising from events clearly distinct from ordinary activities and not expected to recur frequently. Discontinued operations defined as a separate, major line of business that can be clearly distinguished physically, operationally, and for financial reporting purposes. Fundamental errors, relate to prior periods and make past statements unreliable at their date of issue.	Nature and amount of each extraordinary item should be separately disclosed. Nature and amount of all income or expense items that by their size, nature, or incidence are relevant to explain the performance of the enterprise. Nature, segment, effective date, manner of discontinuance, gain or loss and how it is measured; ordinary profit and revenue in all reported periods for the discontinued operations.

Stan-dard No.	Area Covered	Measurement Principles	Disclosure Requirements
		Changes in accounting policies should be made only if required by regulation or if the change will result in a more appropriate presentation of events or transactions.	Fundamental Error: Benchmark: Adjust opening balance and restate prior periods and disclose nature and amounts. Allowed alternative: Adjust current net profit and loss and provide pro forma data consistent with the benchmark. Changes in accounting estimates should be included in current profit and loss and if material the nature and effect disclosed. Changes in accounting policies: Benchmark: Applied retrospectively; adjust opening balances when feasible and disclose reasons for change and past and current amounts affected. Allowed alternative: Applied retrospectively with cumulative adjustment included in the current profit and loss, with reasons for change and amount of adjustment.
9	Research and Development Costs (Re-vised 1993)	Research, defined as original investigation under-taken to gain new scientific or technical knowl-edge and understanding, should be expensed when costs are incurred.	Accounting policies adopted for research and development (R & D) costs. Amount of R & D expensed in the period. Amortization methods and useful lives used. A reconciliation of the change in unamortized development cost asset.

Stan-dard No.	Area Covered	Measurement Principles	Disclosure Requirements
		Development, defined as the application of knowledge to a plan or design for the production of new or substantially improved products, services, etc., prior to commencement of commercial production or use, should be recognized as an expense, unless all of a set of criteria are met in which case the costs should be capitalized and amortized so as to reflect the pattern in which the related benefits are realized. The criteria include: (1) the product/process is technically feasible, (2) the product/process is clearly differentiable, (3) a market exists for the product/process, and (4) resources are available to complete the project.	Development costs allocated to other asset accounts. Development costs previously written off as impaired and written back in the period.
		If capitalized, development costs are subject to an impairment test.	
		All research and development costs are expensed.	
10	Contingencies and Events Occurring After the Balance Sheet Date	A contingent loss should be accrued if it is probable that an asset has been impaired or a liability incurred at a balance sheet date and a reasonable estimate can be made.	If no accrual/write-off is made, the existence of a contingent loss must be disclosed unless possibility of loss is remote. Disclosure should include nature of contingency, related uncertain factors, and estimate of financial effect.
		Contingent gains cannot be recognized.	Existence of contingent gain should be disclosed if it is probable the gain will be realized.
		Post balance sheet date events should be recognized if they relate to the estimation of amounts at the balance sheet date or impact the going-concern assumption.	Nature of post balance sheet event and estimate of financial effect for events that do not affect condition of assets and liabilities at the balance sheet date but for which nondisclosure would affect users' ability to fairly evaluate the financial statement.
		Dividends proposed or declared but not approved should be accrued or disclosed.	

Stan-dard No.	Area Covered	Measurement Principles	Disclosure Requirements
11	Construction Contracts (Revised 1993)	Defines contract revenues and costs and when contract segments can be treated separately or jointly. When the outcome of a construction contract can be estimated reliably (as defined), contract revenue and costs should be recognized as revenue and expenses based on the stage of completion of the contract activity at the balance sheet date. When the outcome cannot be measured reliably, costs should be expensed as incurred and revenue should be recognized to the extent that recovery is probable. When it is probable that contract costs will exceed total contract revenue, the expected loss should be recognized as an expense immediately.	Amount of contract revenue recognized and bases of computation used for the reporting period. Aggregate costs incurred and profits recognized to date, advances received and retentions. Gross amount due from (to) customers as an asset (liability).
12	Accounting for Taxes on Income [Under revision E33 replaced by E49]	Requires accrual of deferred taxes on timing differences plus current taxes. Deferred taxes may be based on the deferral or liability methods and may be excluded when there is reasonable evidence the timing differences will neither reverse for at least three years nor in the foreseeable future (partial method). Net deferred tax assets should not be carried forward unless there is a reasonable expectation of realization.	Tax expenses from ordinary activities and separately disclosed extraordinary items, prior period changes, or changes in accounting policy. Any unaccrued deferred taxes. Method used. Explanation of relation between tax expense and accounting income if not explained by the reporting country's tax rate. Deferred taxes on asset revaluations.

Stand-ard No.	Area Covered	Measurement Principles	Disclosure Requirements
		Tax loss carrybacks are recognized in the period when the loss occurs, and tax loss carryforwards may be accrued if future realization is assured beyond a reasonable doubt, or to the extent they offset other timing differences.	For tax losses, amount of tax saving included in net income from current losses and past loss carryforwards, plus tax loss carryforwards still available for use.
		Taxes due on distribution of undistributed earnings of subsidiaries and associated companies should be accrued unless it is reasonable to assume distribution is unlikely.	Disclose components of income before income taxes as either domestic or foreign and show separately components of income tax expense with amounts of income taxes charged to income from continuing operations and to other sources of income.
		Deferred taxes are based on liability method applied to differences between accounting and tax bases of all assets and liabilities.	Disclose the types and amounts of temporary differences that give rise to significant deferred tax assets or liabilities and disclose temporary differences for which deferred taxes have not been provided. Show also the approximate tax effect of each type of temporary difference. In a footnote, disclose the total of all deferred tax liabilities and deferred tax assets and the total valuation allowance recognized.
13	Presentation of Current Assets and Liabilities	Not relevant	Permits companies to use a current/noncurrent designation if desired but precludes subtotals of assets and liabilities when the classification is not made.
			Details items to include under current assets or liabilities.
			Disclose allowance for doubtful accounts and notes receivable. State separately amount of unearned discounts, finance charges, and interest included in the face amount of receivables.

Stan- dard No.	Area Covered	Measurement Principles	Disclosure Requirements
			Generally, current asset categories in excess of 5% of total current assets must be disclosed separately. In addition, total current assets must be shown.
14	Reporting Financial Information by Segment (under revision)	Not relevant	Report for each economically significant industry or geographical segment: Activity of industry segment. Composition of geographic area. Sales or other operating revenues distinguishing between revenue derived from outside customers and other segments. Segment results. Segment assets employed (either in money amounts or percentages of consolidated totals). Basis of inter-segment pricing. Reconciliation of segment totals to aggregated data reported in the financial statements. Changes in identification of segments and accounting practices used in reporting segment information. By segment, disclose depreciation, depletion and amortization, and capital expenditures. Disclose sales information for aggregate export and significant customers.

Stan- dard No.	Area Covered	Measurement Principles	Disclosure Requirements
15	Information Reflecting the Effects of Changing Prices (not required)		When used: Supplementary information disclosing adjustments to depreciation, cost of sales, net monetary adjustment, current cost of property, plant, and equipment and inventories, and methods used.
16	Property, Plant, and Equipment [PPE] (Revised 1993)	PP&E recognized as an asset at its initial cost when it is probable that future economic benefit will flow to the enterprise and the cost can be measured reliably. Subsequent expenditure relating to an item of PP&E should be capitalized if it will lead to incremental future economic benefit; otherwise, it should be expensed. Benchmark: PP&E carried at (original) cost less accumulated depreciation. Allowed alternative: PP&E carried at revalued amount less accumulated depreciation, with regular revaluation of entire asset class required to ensure fair value at balance sheet date. Revaluation increases taken to revaluation reserve unless offsetting a previous decrease expensed. Revaluation decreases reduce revaluation reserves and are then expensed.	Measurement bases, depreciation methods, and useful lives used. Gross carrying amount and accumulated depreciation at the beginning and end of the period with a reconciliation showing additions, disposals, acquisitions through business combinations, changes from revaluations, impairments and writebacks, depreciation, net translation differences, and other movement. Valuation basis used, effective date, details of valuation, carrying amount on historical basis, revaluation surplus. Whether net present values have been used to determine the recoverable amount.

Stan-dard No.	Area Covered	Measurement Principles	Disclosure Requirements
		Depreciation method should reflect the pattern in which the assets' economic benefits are consumed. Depreciation charge should be recognized as an expense unless it is included in the carrying amount of another asset. Useful life of PP&E and depreciation method used should be reviewed periodically; if expectations are significantly different from previous estimates, the charge for current and future periods should be adjusted. Carrying amount of PP&E should be compared to recoverable amount periodically. Any material reduction should be expensed immediately unless it reverses a previous revaluation, in which case it is set off against the reserve. Subsequent increases in recoverable amount when benchmark treatment is used should be written back (net of depreciation). PP&E should be eliminated from the balance sheet on disposal or permanent retirement from use. Any related gains or losses should be based on the carrying amount and included in the income statement.	Existence and amount of title restrictions or pledge of assets. Accounting policy for restoration costs. Expenditures on account of PP&E in the course of construction. Amount of commitments for acquisition of PP&E. Encouraged disclosures: Carrying amount of temporarily idle PP&E, retired PP&E held for disposal. Gross carrying amount of fully depreciated PP&E still in use. When benchmark treatment is used, the fair value if materially different from the carrying value. State separately the amount of assets held for sale or investment.

Stan-dard No.	Area Covered	Measurement Principles	Disclosure Requirements
17	Accounting for Leases	For lessee: Finance lease recorded as an asset and liability at lower of fair value (net of grants and tax credits to lessor) or present value of minimum lease payments based on implicit interest rate or lessee's incremental borrowing rate. Lease payments should be allocated to finance charge and principal payments with assets being depreciated. Lessees should recognize lease expense on operating leases on a systematic basis representative of user's benefit. For lessor: Lessor should treat net investment in lease as a receivable with finance charge based on a constant periodic rate. Manufacturer/dealer lessor should recognize profit on sale as if a normal sale. Lessor should treat assets held for operating leases as PP&E, with rental income recognized straight line over the life of the lease unless another systematic pattern is more consistent with the earnings process. Profits on sales and leaseback transactions treated as finance leases should be deferred and amortized over life of lease. If treated as an operating lease, income can be recognized if the transaction is established at fair value; otherwise gains/losses should be deferred and amortized. A lease is a finance lease if it transfers to the lessee substantially all the risks and rewards incident to ownership.	For lessee: Amount of assets and liabilities that are the subject of finance leases at each balance sheet date. Commitments for minimum lease payments with a term of more than one year, in summary form showing amounts and periods when due. Significant financing restrictions, renewal or purchase options, contingent rentals and other contingencies. For lessor: Gross investment in leases and related unearned finance income and unguaranteed residual value for finance leases. Basis used for allocating income to provide a constant periodic rate of return. Amounts of assets and related accumulated depreciation for each class of assets held as operating leases. Additional disclosures regarding future minimum lease payments and contingent rentals.

Stan-dard No.	Area Covered	Measurement Principles	Disclosure Requirements
18	Revenue (Revised 1993)	Revenue (as defined) measured at fair value of consideration received or receivable.	Accounting policies used, including method to determine stage of completion.
		Revenue recognized when all the following conditions are met:	Amount of each significant category of revenue recognized, including revenue from:
		Significant risks and rewards of ownership of the goods have been transferred to buyer.	sale of goods
		No continuing managerial control nor effective control over goods sold.	rendering of services
		Amount of revenue and costs incurred can be measured reliably.	interest
		Economic benefits from the transaction will probably flow to the enterprise.	royalties
		For services rendered, revenue recognized based on stage of completion at balance sheet date when outcome can be reliably measured (as defined). If outcome cannot be reliably measured, revenue recognized to the extent of expenses.	dividends
		Interest recognized on basis of effective yield and proportion of time.	Revenue arising from exchange of goods and services included in each category.
		Royalties recognized on an accrual basis.	
		Dividends recognized when right to receive payment is established.	

Stan-dard No.	Area Covered	Measurement Principles	Disclosure Requirements

19	Retirement Benefit Costs (Revised 1993) [Does not yet specifically cover other post-employment benefits; under revision to broaden]	*Defined Contribution Plans:*
		
		Contribution recognized as an expense in period of contribution.
		
		Defined Benefit Plans:
		
		Current service cost recognized as expense in period when service rendered.
		
		Past service costs, experience adjustments, effect of changes in actuarial assumptions, and effects of plan amendments for existing employees in the plan should be recognized as income or expense systematically over the expected remaining working lives of the employees except if there is no future economic benefit anticipated.
		
		For probable plan termination, curtailments, or settlement any increase in cost should be expensed when probable but any gain should be recognized as income when the event occurs.
		
		For retired employees, effect of plan amendment recognized as income or expense when amendment is made.
		
		Actuarial valuation method:
		
		Benchmark:
		  Accrued benefit method, i.e., based on services rendered.
		
		Allowed alternative:
		  Project benefit method, i.e., based on services rendered and to be rendered.
			General description of plan, including employees covered, amount recognized as an expense, and other significant items.
			
			General description of the plan, including employees covered.
			
			Accounting policies adopted, including actuarial valuation methods and assumptions used.
			
			Whether plan is funded and fair value of plan assets.
			
			Amount recognized as income or expense.
			
			Most recent actuarial present value of promised retirement benefits.
			
			Any under- or overfunded plans and funding approach adopted.
			
			Any significant changes in actuarial assumptions.
			
			Date of most recent actuarial valuation and frequency with which valuations are made.
			
			Any other matters that affect comparability, including the effects of plan termination, curtailment, or settlement.
			
			Extensive disclosure information is required.

Standard No.	Area Covered	Measurement Principles	Disclosure Requirements
		Actuarial assumptions: Appropriate and compatible assumptions incorporating projected salary levels to retirement should be used.	
		Specific actuarial methods are required.	
20	Accounting for Government Grants and Disclosure of Government Assistance	Government grants should not be recognized until there is reasonable assurance that the enterprise will comply with the conditions attaching to them and the grants will be received.	Accounting policy adopted, nature and extent of government grants recognized in the financial statements, and other forms of government assistance that have provided direct benefits.
		Grants should not be credited directly to shareholders' interests but matched against related costs through the income statement and set up as deferred income or deducted from the carrying amount of the assets.	Unfulfilled conditions and other contingencies relating to government assistance recognized.
		Government grants receivable for past expenses or losses should be recognized as unusual income when it becomes receivable, if appropriate.	
		Government grants that become repayable should be treated as a change in accounting estimates.	

Stan-dard No.	Area Covered	Measurement Principles	Disclosure Requirements
21	The Effects of Changes in Foreign Exchange Rates	*Transactions:* Recorded on initial recognition by applying the spot exchange rate. At each subsequent balance sheet date. For foreign currency monetary items, use closing rate; for nonmonetary items carried at historical cost (fair value) in foreign currency, use historical (fair value date) exchange rate. Benchmark: Exchange differences arising from transactions not deemed as a part or hedge of a net investment should be recognized as income/expense in the period they arise. Exchange differences on monetary items that in substance form part of net investment in a foreign entity or accounted for as a hedge of that net investment should be classified as equity until disposal of the net investment. Allowed alternative: Exchange differences from severe devaluations that cannot be hedged and arise directly from the recent acquisition of an asset invoiced in a foreign currency can be included in the cost of the asset provided that the adjusted carrying amount does not exceed lower of replacement cost and recoverable amount.	Amount of exchange differences in net profit or loss. Amount of exchange difference included in carrying value of an asset in accordance with the allowed alternative.

Stan-dard No.	Area Covered	Measurement Principles	Disclosure Requirements
		Translation of Statements of Foreign Operations:	Net exchange differences classified as equity, including reconciliation of beginning and ending balances.
		If foreign operation is integral to the operations of the reporting enterprise, then treat as if all transactions are those of the reporting enterprise with all resulting gains and losses included in net profit or loss.	Accounting policy for translation of goodwill and fair value adjustments arising on the acquisition of a foreign entity
		If foreign operations reflect a separate operating entity (as defined), except if operating in a hyperinflationary economy:	
		All assets and liabilities translated at closing rate.	
		Income and expense items translated at transaction date exchange rates.	
		All resulting exchange differences classified as equity until disposal of the net investment.	
		If foreign entity operates in a hyperinflationary environment, then financial statements should be restated in accordance with IAS 29 and then translated at closing rates.	
		On disposal of a foreign entity, the cumulative translation difference deferred in equity should be recognized as income or expense.	

Stan-dard No.	Area Covered	Measurement Principles	Disclosure Requirements
22	Business Combinations (Revised 1993)	An acquisition occurs when the acquirer obtains control over the net assets and operations of another enterprise as a result of an exchange.	For all business combinations: Names and descriptions of combining enterprises. Method of accounting for and the effective date of the combination.
		For an acquisition, from the date of acquisition the acquirer should incorporate results of operations, individual assets and liabilities of the acquiree, and recognize any goodwill.	Any operations resulting from the combination that the enterprise has decided to dispose of.
		Acquisition cost is based on amount of any cash and fair value at date of exchange of any other purchase consideration, plus acquisition costs.	For year of acquisition in purchases: Percentage of voting shares acquired. Cost of acquisition and a description of the purchase consideration payable.
		Benchmark: The assets and liabilities are measured at fair value for the acquirer's portion plus the minority's proportion at pre-acquisition carrying amount.	Nature and amount of provisions for restructuring and other plant closure expenses arising as result of acquisition and recognized at that time.
		Allowed alternative: The assets and liabilities are measured at fair value.	Accounting treatment of goodwill, amortization period with justification when greater than five years and when straight line is not used, a reconciliation of period's goodwill (negative goodwill) including gross amounts, accumulated and current amortization, additions, changes in value during the period.
		Any excess of acquisition cost over acquirer's interest in the fair value of the identifiable assets and liabilities acquired is goodwill, which must be recognized as an asset and amortized over its useful life, which should not exceed five years unless a longer period, not exceeding twenty years, can be justified. Unamortized goodwill should be reviewed at each period and if no longer probable of being recovered should be recognized immediately as an expense.	If provisional values used, describe reasons plus subsequent changes.
			State separately any intangible assets in amounts greater than 5% of total assets. Also disclose the basis of valuation and explain significant additions or deletions.
			Full year pro forma results of operations for periods including a business combination accounted for as a purchase.

Stan-dard No.	Area Covered	Measurement Principles	Disclosure Requirements
		Negative Goodwill:	
		Benchmark:	
		When cost of acquisition is less than acquirer's interest in the fair value of identifiable net assets acquired, the fair values of acquired nonmonetary assets should be reduced proportionately until the excess is eliminated. Any excess is described as negative goodwill and recognized as income in a manner equivalent to goodwill.	
		Allowed alternative:	
		Any excess in acquirer's share of fair value of net assets acquired is described as negative goodwill and recognized as income in a manner equivalent to goodwill.	
		Contingent purchase considerations should be included in acquisition cost if the adjustment is probable and can be measured reliably. Thereafter, adjustments will be made as the two conditions are met.	
		Adjustment to the fair value of assets and liabilities acquired can be included in acquisition cost up to the end of the first annual accounting period commencing after acquisition; otherwise, such adjustments must be treated as income or expense.	
		Goodwill is amortized over a period not to exceed 40 years.	

Stan-dard No.	Area Covered	Measurement Principles	Disclosure Requirements
		A Uniting of Interest occurs when the shareholders of the combining enterprises combine control to achieve a continuing sharing in the risks and rewards of the combined entity.	For Uniting of Interest: Description and number of shares issued, together with percentage of voting shares exchanged.
		A Uniting of Interest should be accounted for as a pooling of interests whereby the financial statements of the uniting interests are combined from the earliest period presented.	Amounts of assets and liabilities contributed by each enterprise. Operating revenues, extraordinary items, and net profit or loss of each enterprise prior to date of combinations and included in combined enterprises financial statements.
		Any difference between consideration made and amount recorded for share capital acquired should be adjusted against equity.	
23	Borrowing Costs (Revised 1993)	Benchmark: Recognize as an expense in the period in which the costs are incurred.	Accounting policy used. Amount of borrowing costs capitalized and capitalization rate used.
		Allowed alternative: Borrowing costs directly attributable to the acquisition, construction, or production of a qualifying asset should be capitalized as part of the cost of that asset; all other borrowing costs should be expensed.	
		For specific borrowings, net interest is capitalized.	
		For general borrowings, apply a capitalization rate based on weighted average of applicable borrowing costs to the borrowing costs applied to expenditures on the asset.	

Stan-dard No.	Area Covered	Measurement Principles	Disclosure Requirements
		Capitalization of borrowing costs commences when expenditures for the asset and borrowing costs are being incurred and activities necessary to prepare the asset for use are in progress. Capitalization is suspended when active development is interrupted and ceased when all activities necessary to prepare the asset for use or sale are complete.	
24	Related Party Disclosures	Not relevant	Related party relationships where control exists, even if no transactions between them. For transactions between related parties (as defined) disclose nature of relationship, elements, and types of transactions.
25	Accounting for Investments (will be impacted by outcome of Financial Instruments E48)	Investments classified as current assets should be carried at either market value or the lower of cost and market value, which can be determined either on a portfolio or individual investment basis. When market value is used, the increases or decreases can be included in income or gains can be included in equity as a revaluation surplus and any subsequent decrease may be set off such a surplus.	Accounting policies for: Determination of carrying amounts. Treatment of changes in market value and/or revaluation surplus. Significant amounts included in income for interest; royalties, dividends, and rentals; profits and losses on disposal; and changes in values of investments. Market value of investments if not carried at market and fair value of investment properties if not carried at fair value. Any significant restrictions on realizability of investments or related income.

Stan-dard No.	Area Covered	Measurement Principles	Disclosure Requirements
		Investments classified as long-term assets should be carried at either cost, revalued amounts, or the lower of cost or market value on a portfolio basis. If revaluations are used, a policy for frequency of revaluations must be adopted. Declines in carrying amount other than of a temporary nature must be reflected.	For revalued long-term investments: Policy and frequency of revaluations. Date and basis of last revaluation. Movement and nature of revaluation surplus. For enterprises whose main business is holding of investment, an analysis of the portfolio.
		Revaluations of long-term investments reflecting increases should be treated as a revaluation surplus in equity, with subsequent declines of same investment set off against the surplus. In all other cases, declines should be charged to income.	Disclose any material change from the preceding period in the entities included or excluded in consolidation.
		Gains/losses on sale of investments should be based on carrying values and reported in income.	
		For fiscal years beginning after December 15, 1993, securities are classified in three categories and accounted for as follows:	
		Debt securities to be held-to-maturity are carried at amortized cost.	
		Debt and equity securities bought for the purpose of selling are classified as trading securities and are carried at fair value with unrealized gains and losses included in earnings.	
		Other securities are classified as available for sale securities and are reported at fair value with unrealized gains and losses excluded from earnings and reported in a separate component of shareholders' equity.	

Stan-dard No.	Area Covered	Measurement Principles	Disclosure Requirements
26	Accounting and Reporting by Retirement Benefit Plans	Actual present value of promised benefits based on services rendered to date and either current or projected salary levels. Benefit plan investments carried at fair value.	A statement showing net assets available for benefits, actuarial present value of promised vested and non-vested benefits, and resulting excess or deficit. If a current actuarial valuation is not available, then the most recent valuation should be used with date of valuation disclosed. Basis of salary levels used. If fair value not used for plan benefits, explanation required. Funding policy. Statement of changes in net assets available, significant accounting policies, description of the plan, and changes thereto.
27	Consolidated Financial Statements and Accounting for Investments in Subsidiaries	Consolidated financial statements to be presented except by wholly owned subsidiaries. All subsidiaries included except if control is temporary because acquired and held for subsequent disposal, or if subsidiary operates under long-term restrictions that impair ability to transfer funds to parent. Prepared using uniform practices, adjusted to equivalent reporting dates, intragroup balances, transactions, and unrealized profits to be eliminated.	Minority interest presented separately with share in net assets separated from liabilities and parent shareholders' equity. Reasons for not consolidating a subsidiary. Nature of relationship if parent does not own directly or indirectly more than one half of voting power but which because of absence of control is not a subsidiary. Effect of acquisition/disposition of subsidiaries on financial position and results of the current and preceding periods. Separate financial statements are required for significant acquired businesses. Disclose any material change from the preceding period in the entities consolidated.

Stan- dard No.	Area Covered	Measurement Principles	Disclosure Requirements
28	Accounting for Invest- ments in Associates	An investment in an associate (defined in terms of significant influence) is accounted for under equity method unless acquired and held for disposal in the near future. Equity method to be discontinued when significant influence ceases or the associate operates under severe restrictions impairing ability to transfer funds to investor. Carrying amount of an investment in an associate should be reduced to recognize a nontemporary decline in the investment.	A listing and description of significant associates, including the proportion of ownership interest and voting power held. Methods used to account for associates. If equity accounting is used, the investments should be classified as a separate item of long-term assets and disclosed as a separate item in the income statement. The investor's share of unusual or prior period items should also be disclosed separately. Provide separate financial statements for signifi-cant less-than-majority-owned subsidiaries (as defined in SEC Regulations). Also, provide separate financial statements for businesses acquired or to be acquired if those businesses are significant. Disclose differences, if any, between carrying value and amount of underlying equity in net assets and accounting treatment of the difference. Also show investor's share of extraordinary items and prior period adjustments unless they are immaterial and material subsequent events. Disclose aggregate market values of each investment if available. Also disclose names of significant investees in which less than 20% is held and the reason for using the equity method, and names of significant investees in which more than 20% is held and the reason for not using the equity method.

Stan-dard No.	Area Covered	Measurement Principles	Disclosure Requirements
29	Financial Reporting in Hyper-inflationary Economies	Financial statements of an enterprise reporting in the currency of a hyperinflationary economy should be stated in the measuring unit current at the balance sheet date. Information from earlier periods should be similarly restated. The net gain or loss on the net monetary position should be included in net income and separately disclosed. When the economy is no longer hyperinflationary, then the amounts expressed in the measuring unit current at the end of the previous reporting period is the basis for the carrying amount going forward. Financial statements of an enterprise reporting in the currency of a hyperinflationary economy shall be remeasured as if the functional currency were the reporting currency. (Eliminated by SEC December 1994)	The fact that restatement has occurred, its nature, and identify levels of index used. Whether financial statements are based on historical or current costs.
30	Disclosures in the Financial Statements of Banks and Similar Financial Institutions	No set off of assets and liabilities unless legal right of set off exists and the offsetting represents expected realization or settlement.	Income statement should group income and expense items by nature and disclose the amounts of the principal types. In addition to other IAS requirements, specific disclosures specified highlighting key elements of balance sheet and income statement. Detailed commitments and contingencies are specified and must be disclosed. Maturity groupings of assets and liabilities.

Stan-dard No.	Area Covered	Measurement Principles	Disclosure Requirements
			Concentrations of assets and liabilities and off-balance sheet items, in term of geographical areas, customer or industry groups, or other concentrations of risk.
			Amount of significant net foreign currency exposure.
			Policy and details relating to loan loss provisions and nonperforming assets.
			Pledged assets.
31	Financial Reporting of Interests in Joint Ventures	*Jointly Controlled Operations:* A venturer recognizes assets it controls, liabilities and expenses it incurs, and its share of the income earned.	Various contingencies (as detailed).
		Jointly Controlled Assets: A venturer recognizes its share of the assets (appropriately classified), liabilities incurred or its share thereof, any income from sale or use of its share of output, its share of expenses, plus any expenses it has incurred.	Aggregate amounts of capital commitments relating to the venture.
			A listing and description of interests in significant ventures and the proportion of ownership interest held in each jointly controlled entity.
		Jointly Controlled Entities: In a venturer's consolidated financial statements: Benchmark: Report its interests using proportionate consolidation. Allowed alternative: Use the equity method.	Aggregate amounts of current assets, long-term assets, current liabilities, long-term liabilities, income, and expenses related to its interest in joint ventures.
			Proportionate consolidation is normally not acceptable for US-GAAP; however, the SEC does not require that it be shown as a reconciling item. Need to disclose summarized information relating to the balance sheet, income statement, and statement of cash flows.

Stan-dard No.	Area Covered	Measurement Principles	Disclosure Requirements
		Unless the interest is acquired and held exclusively for sale or the jointly controlled entity operates under severe long-term restrictions limiting transfer of funds.	
		Transactions between a venturer and joint venture should be treated similarly to intragroup transactions.	

In addition to the standards listed, the IASC has two exposure drafts outstanding: E48 on Financial Instruments and E49 on Income Taxes.

Other projects currently being revised or written include: Segment Reporting, Earnings per Share, Intangible Assets, Presentation of Financial Statements, and Retirement Benefit Costs

Note:

1. This table is not intended to represent a comprehensive checklist, but rather summarizes the key requirements. The shaded areas reflect the material additional requirements for non-US registrants under Item 18 of Form 20-F.

Appendix B

Summary of Detailed Analyses for Each Sample Company

The analyses in this appendix are based on the financial statements of the year analyzed and hence may differ from the current practice of the reported companies. There will also be new standards under US-GAAP which would not have been incorporated.

B-1 The Atlas Copco Group

OVERVIEW

Atlas Copco is a Swedish multinational operating in the areas of compressor, construction and mining, and industrial engineering (technique). The majority of its revenues are generated outside Sweden. Atlas Copco had 48 manufacturing plants in 15 countries at the time of the 1992 annual report, which was used in the study. Most of the sales occur in the European Union and North America. At the time of the analysis, Atlas Copco's shares were listed on the Stockholm, London, and three German stock exchanges. The ten largest shareholders control 60 percent of the voting rights and 51 percent of the shares outstanding. The largest shareholder is Investor. In the 1992 annual report, Atlas Copco presents its financial statements in accordance with Swedish GAAP. It also presents summary reconciliations to IAS and US-GAAP for several items. In 1992, Atlas Copco adopted several changes in accounting principles which reduced the variations from both IAS and US-GAAP. Atlas Copco was not audited by Coopers & Lybrand but appointed Coopers & Lybrand as joint auditors in 1994.

SPECIFIC DIFFERENCES

A. Acquisitions, Business Combinations, and Consolidations

In 1992, Atlas Copco adjusted its accounting policy for goodwill. Historically, goodwill arising from "strategic acquisitions" was amortized "at a real amortization rate," increasing with inflation. This practice was changed to amortization on a straight-line basis, over 20 years, the maximum permitted under a new Swedish principle. The cumulative effect of the accounting change was to increase goodwill by SEK 39 million with a related SEK 5 million reduction in deferred tax liabilities. These amounts are not disclosed separately in the Swedish GAAP accounts. Goodwill from nonstrategic acquisitions is amortized over 10 years because of their shorter economic life. The current amortization policy is considered to be consistent with IAS and US-GAAP.

Atlas Copco accounted for its acquisition of the Secoroc Group in 1988 as a pooling of interests as permitted under Swedish GAAP and IAS at that time. The acquisition does not qualify as a pooling of interests under US-GAAP, nor as a "uniting of interest" under the revised IAS. Applying the maximum 40-year amortization period to the goodwill, as allowed under US-GAAP, would result in a decrease in income of SEK 12 million and an increase in shareholders' equity of approximately SEK 472 million. Revised IAS do not require retroactive adjustments, but the maximum amortization period under IAS is 20 years. If Atlas Copco were to apply the 20-year rule consistently, the shareholders' equity would be increased by SEK 428 million. In addition, if the pooling-of-interests method was eliminated and replaced by purchase accounting, other components of the balance sheet and income statement would change by varying amounts as a result of the write-up to fair value at the acquisition date. For this project, it is not feasible to restate the values of the components accurately, and any such measurement would have no impact on the US-GAAP reconciliations of earnings and shareholders' equity.

Atlas Copco reevaluates the economic life of its assets annually to assess whether the goodwill amortization is adequate, and makes adjustments if necessary. This is consistent with revised IAS and the current policy of the SEC, although no official goodwill impairment standard exists currently within US-GAAP.

All acquisitions other than the Secoroc Group, previously discussed, were accounted for as acquisitions with net assets written up to fair value. The net amounts of write-ups and related amortization, by category, are shown in the notes to the accounts. Thus, the disclosures are consistent with both IAS and US-GAAP.

One acquisition resulted in net negative goodwill and equity (after writing down tangible assets). This negative goodwill would be amortized under US-GAAP and revised IAS and would have caused an immaterial increase in income in 1992. At the end of 1992, there was no remaining balance of negative goodwill.

Associate companies in which Atlas Copco owns between 20 and 50 percent of the voting rights and has significant influence are accounted for on an equity basis beginning in 1992. The cumulative effect of the accounting change increased income by SEK 16 million, is adjusted retroactively, and is not separately disclosed.

B. Foreign Currency Translation

For entities operating in nonhyperinflationary environments, Atlas Copco uses a current rate approach consistent with SFAS 52 and IAS 21. However, because of the way Swedish GAAP requires company and group accounts to split restricted and unrestricted reserves, the company has not split out the currency translation effects from each reserve so as to reflect an aggregate cumulative translation adjustment as required under IAS and US-GAAP. If a subsidiary is sold, no transfer of the cumulative translation adjustment is taken to income. As there has been no significant disposal of a business in the recent past, this does not present a practical problem so far. There is no direct effect on shareholders' equity, merely on the components, and a non-US registrant with the SEC would not be required to present a shareholders' equity account classified on a US-GAAP basis in Form 20-F.

In the case of subsidiaries operating in hyperinflationary environments, the company has two approaches. The Brazilian subsidiary price-level-adjusts its accounts, which are then translated first into US dollars and then into Swedish kronor. This is consistent with revised IAS but not US-GAAP at the time. The SEC accepted this approach for non-US registrants in December 1994. For all other subsidiaries operating in hyperinflationary economies, Atlas Copco uses the US dollar as functional currency. The SEC has usually enforced using the reporting currency as the functional currency for group companies that operate in hyperinflationary economies and invoice their sales in the local currency. This policy would require the use of the kronor as the functional currency. While the SEC's approach is consistent with SFAS 52, the use of the US dollar as functional currency can be viewed as consistent with the economic substance and arguably with SFAS 52 and IAS 21. For this project, it was not financially feasible to quantify the difference that using the kronor as functional currency would cause.

A final issue related to foreign currency items is the policy on hedging. Atlas Copco may enter into contracts to hedge sales anticipated to occur within the following six months. Gains and losses under such contracts are deferred, while they would be recorded as income (expense) under US-GAAP unless there is a firm commitment.[1] This difference is not quantified, but it is believed to have an immaterial effect on income in any one year, as the policy is applied consistently and year-to-year changes in the quantities involved are small. IAS is currently silent on this issue, though some resolution to the financial instruments project (E48) is forthcoming. Based on the current proposal, the Atlas Copco treatment is acceptable.

---

1 Currently, US-GAAP treats foreign currency hedges and other financial instrument hedges inconsistently in terms of the treatment for certain anticipated contracts (Herz [1994]).

C. Shareholders' Equity

As mentioned, Swedish GAAP restricts certain equity from distribution to shareholders. The classification into restricted reserves and retained earnings differs from the components required under IAS and US-GAAP. No attempt was made to revise the IAS/US-GAAP components, as the reclassification would have no impact on the aggregate equity. Similarly, while Atlas Copco presents disclosures of the movements in these accounts, the presentation differs somewhat from that required in the statement of changes in shareholders' equity required by IAS and US-GAAP.

D. Property, Plant, and Equipment

Swedish companies are permitted to revalue land and buildings up to a certain level. While no revaluation has occurred for many years, Atlas Copco has a balance remaining from past revaluations. IAS permits revaluations of assets as an allowed alternative, but US-GAAP requires use of historical costs. The adjustment to historical cost is essentially immaterial as it would increase income by SEK 1 million and reduce shareholders' equity by SEK 31 million.

US-GAAP requires capitalization of interest (borrowing costs) under certain circumstances. Atlas Copco complies with Swedish GAAP and does not capitalize interest. In general, this item is not material and there was no effect on net income in 1992. The cumulative effect, which increases shareholders' equity, is SEK 76 million.

Revised IAS requires capitalization of development costs once a product reaches a stage of viability. Atlas Copco expenses all its research and development costs, which is consistent with US-GAAP. The nature of Atlas Copco's business and the stringent conditions set out in IAS 9 (as revised) for capitalization of development costs suggest that Atlas Copco's practice is materially consistent with both US-GAAP and IAS.

Atlas Copco does not capitalize any noncancelable operating leases, nor does it provide a schedule of payments. However, it discloses the present value of all noncancelable operating leases as well as the value of the underlying assets subject to leasing. Thus, the economic substance of the disclosures required under IAS and US-GAAP is provided. The management believes that no material amount of the operating leases would qualify for capitalization under either IAS or US-GAAP.

E. Investments

Atlas Copco has an actively traded portfolio of marketable securities that is continually marked to market, which is acceptable under IAS. The portfolio is constantly being turned over, so it is probable that the market value approximates historical cost. While US-GAAP applied a lower of cost and market value rule through 1992, Atlas Copco's practice is consistent with current US-GAAP. Any potential adjustment to historic cost would be immaterial.

"Other investments" to be held to maturity are shown at cost. In 1992, the market value may have been slightly lower, but no adjustment to a contra-equity account (as required by US-GAAP) or income (as possible under IAS) was made. Any adjustment would have been immaterial, so this potential difference was ignored.

The group does not provide the disclosures of financial instruments currently required by US-GAAP and in the proposed IAS (E48). However, it includes in its contingent liabilities any potential exposures if counterparties do not deliver on the derivative contracts. Hence, while additional disclosures are required, at the time of the 1992 annual report the disclosures were essentially consistent with US-GAAP.

F. Discontinued Operations and Changes in Accounting Policies

As mentioned, Atlas Copco does not disclose the cumulative effect of accounting changes separately.

G. Taxation

Historically, Sweden has had several "tax-free" reserves which may still exist in the separate legal entities. However, for group reporting purposes, all reserves are split into equity and the potential tax added to deferred tax. This would include taxes applicable to temporary differences arising from tax versus book (cost) depreciation. Hence, the historical issue of tax-based reserves no longer applies.

In Sweden, there has been a tax deduction available on the payment of dividends for a period after the issue of new shares. This "Annell deduction" was utilized in 1992. However, the deduction is being eliminated and it is not available unless certain future actions occur. Hence, no deferred taxes are created for this item. This is considered to be consistent with IAS and US-GAAP, although US accounting firms are currently considering such situations to recommend to the EITF what the appropriate treatment should be. Nevertheless, under IAS and US-GAAP, one would expect to see more disclosure explaining the entire issue.

One tax practice in which Swedish GAAP differs from both IAS and US-GAAP is that the tax expense related to the accrual of income for investments accounted for on an equity basis is shown as part of tax expense. That is, the equity income is incorporated on a pretax basis with the tax included in the tax expense. This is a reclassification item and has no impact on net income or shareholders' equity. In 1992, this tax expense was SEK 14 million.

The group does not describe the differences between tax and accounting values of all assets and liabilities, as required currently under SFAS 109 and partially proposed in E49. However, SFAS 109 was not in effect in 1992. The group does not disclose any reconciliation between statutory and effective tax rates.

H. Post-Employment Benefits

Atlas Copco's primary defined benefit plans are found in Sweden, Germany, and the United States. Each country's pension obligation is accounted for on the basis of that country's GAAP. In Sweden, the obligation is based on current salary levels, but discounted at a real (as opposed to nominal) interest rate. If wage rates change at the rate of inflation, then this will be equivalent to considering future salary increases, and in this sense it will be consistent with IAS and US-GAAP. The actuarial calculations for most of the Swedish obligation are performed by a national organization administering pension plans [Pension registrerings institutet (FPG/PRI)]. Hence, for this exercise it is impractical to estimate differences to US-GAAP, which may exist. There are no plan assets for these plans.

The US companies accrue their pension obligations in conformity with US-GAAP, which is consistent with IAS. However, at the end of 1992 no provision had been made for other post-employment benefits. Companies were only required to accrue this item in 1993. The net effect on 1992 income, other than the cumulative effect of the change in policy, would have been a SEK 6 million reduction. The total effect on shareholders' equity would have been a decrease of SEK 100 million at December 31, 1992.

For German subsidiaries, the provisions are made in accordance with German tax laws. It is likely that there is a slight under-accrual relative to IAS and US-GAAP as a result of nonconsideration of future salary increases. There may be additional differences relative to US-GAAP as a result of other actuarial assumptions, but these are unlikely to be material given the relative size of the German operations.

Based on a relative cost-benefit perspective, no quantification of the adequacy of the pension accruals, relative to the requirements of US-GAAP, was attempted.

Atlas Copco does not give the detailed disclosure of pension costs required under US-GAAP and revised IAS 19. However, it does highlight one component being the portion relating to interest on the liability. In accordance with Swedish GAAP, the company includes this interest as part of financial expense. IAS and US-GAAP classify such costs as part of the pension expense, which is an operating expense. However, the information is clearly available for any user wishing to make an adjustment, and would have no impact on income or shareholders' equity.

There is no disclosure of any plan assets. However, these are likely to exist only in the US subsidiaries.

I. Revenue Recognition

While Atlas Copco's stated policy is use of a completed contract basis, there are no significant long-term contracts at the time of the 1992 annual report. Both IAS and US-GAAP require use of a percentage of completion method, hence an adjustment would have been required if long-term contracts existed.

J. Segment Reporting

The company provides several disclosures on segment sales and other items in various parts of the annual report. The primary component required by IAS and US-GAAP and not provided by the company is the operating income by geographical segment. US-GAAP also requires disclosure of depreciation by line-of-business.

K. Related Party Transactions

Management indicated that all such transactions were disclosed.

L. Statement of Cash Flows

Atlas Copco provides a statement of changes in financial position and not a cash flow statement as required under revised IAS and US-GAAP.

M. Other Items

The narrative surrounding the financial statements contains most of the information contained in a management discussion and analysis section. In general, the disclosures by Atlas Copco are quite detailed. Furthermore, the income statement is in a more summarized form than in an IAS or US-GAAP statement, but the detailed information is provided in the notes.

SUMMARY

Atlas Copco's 1992 annual report won the prize for having the best annual report in Sweden. This is reflected in the findings that most items do not differ materially from either IAS or US-GAAP, which is also a result of the significant changes in certain accounting policies in 1992. Some of the key differences that remain relate to a past acquisition treated as a pooling, revalued assets, and interest capitalization. These differences have been disclosed in the notes to Atlas Copco's financial statements for 1992. There are certain additional disclosures required, including a cash flow statement instead of the statement of changes in financial position presented.

B-2 The Bayer Group

OVERVIEW

The Bayer Group operates in the chemical, pharmaceutical, and imaging technology fields with operations throughout the world, and a particularly heavy concentration in Europe and North America. The group is headquartered in Germany and so presents its financial statements in accordance with German GAAP on December 31, 1993, the fiscal year-end used in this study.[1] Consequently, this analysis presents reconciliations first to revised IAS and then to US-GAAP. At the outset, it is worth noting that several items are included in the German financial statements because of German law, even though they are completely immaterial. The lack of materiality would lead to their exclusion from IAS and US-GAAP statements. While the adjustments reported here were not audited, all the data provided by the company are from working schedules, which had been audited at the time of this analysis. Bayer's shares are listed in Frankfurt, London, Tokyo, and several other exchanges. It completed a survey of shareholders in 1993 and found no single holding in excess of 5%. The shares were also widely held geographically.

SPECIFIC DIFFERENCES

A. Acquisitions, Business Combinations, and Consolidations

In the consolidated financial statements, Bayer includes a number of subsidiaries and associated companies at their cost rather than consolidating them as

---

1 While it is conceivable that German companies can adopt IAS and still conform to German GAAP, this approach was not adopted by Bayer in 1993.

required, in principle, under IAS and US-GAAP. These are immaterial in every respect and are excluded to save administrative costs; hence they have no impact on the usefulness of the financial statements. In addition, as a result of their immaterial nature, 12 nonconsolidated subsidiaries are accounted for on an equity basis rather than fully consolidated. The reason these are included on an equity basis, while others are on a cost basis, is that previously the subsidiaries had been material and consolidated. Once they became small, the cumulative post-acquisition profits that had been accrued were not reversed, so the investments are included on an equity basis. Therefore, no adjustment would be required under IAS or US-GAAP.

Like many other European companies, Bayer uses proportional consolidation for two joint ventures. This treatment would be retained under IAS but, at that time, not under US-GAAP, which requires use of equity accounting. There is no effect on income and shareholders' equity. The joint ventures account for 1.9% of sales, 1.4% of assets, and 1.8% of liabilities in 1993. The SEC now allows non-US registrants to use proportional consolidation.

Bayer calculates the premium (goodwill) on acquisition of subsidiaries as the difference between the purchase price and fair value of net assets acquired. Historically, this goodwill has been written off against shareholders' equity in the year of acquisition. This was acceptable under IAS but is not acceptable under revised IAS, nor under US-GAAP. The major acquisitions for which goodwill existed before the write-off occurred from 1988 onwards. The net book value remaining, assuming a 20-year life for the largest acquisitions, is DM1,116.7 million and goodwill amortization in 1993 would have been DM73.5 million. Note that this adjustment would not have to be made under revised IAS because of the concession not to retroactively adjust for the revised standards. Additional disclosures would be required for major acquisitions.

B. Foreign Currency Translation

Two issues arise in this context, accounting for specific transactions and translation of the accounts of non-German subsidiaries. German law does not allow for the recognition of unrealized foreign exchange gains on transaction balances. Both IAS and US-GAAP require recognition of these unrealized gains. The amount of unrealized gains was DM12 million in 1993 and DM15 million in 1992. Hence, the impact on net income is marginal (DM3 million after-tax).

A related issue arises in the context of receivables that are hedged (primarily with forward contracts). Bayer translates these balances at the hedged rate (e.g., forward rate). This results in recognition of unrealized gains related to forward contracts, which is consistent with IAS and US-GAAP. However, translating foreign currency balances at the spot rate, at the inception of the contract (as required by IAS and US-GAAP), leads to a difference between forward and spot rates that should be amortized over the life of the contract, not recognized immediately as Bayer does. This difference will vary from period to period, but is not material in the normal course of business, including at fiscal year-end 1993.

German law has no requirements with respect to foreign currency translation. Bayer uses historical (average) rates for its long-lived nonmonetary assets, including investments. Other balance sheet accounts and net income are translated at the year-end (current) rate. The income and expense components of income are translated at a weighted average rate.[2]

The net foreign currency translation adjustment is taken to shareholders' equity, although an adjustment is made in operating income for the difference between the year-end and weighted average rates. While these methods approximate a DM as functional currency approach, Bayer believes that all material subsidiaries are independent (rather than integrated) entities. Consequently, under IAS and US-GAAP, it would apply the current rather than historic rate to the long-lived assets. In addition, under revised IAS 21 and US-GAAP, it would not adjust net income to year-end rates. This income adjustment increased net income by DM47 million in 1993, with a cumulative effect from 1987 through 1993 of DM63 million. There were larger adjustments prior to 1987, but these were based on statements prepared under the old law and are not directly comparable. Further, the cumulative effect is simply a reallocation between reported retained earnings and the cumulative translation adjustment.

The cumulative translation adjustment will also be adjusted for the translation effects of using historic versus current exchange rates for fixed assets, which has a cumulative effect of DM429 million at year-end 1993. Thus, assets and equity would be written down by this amount.[3]

C. Shareholders' Equity

German companies have been perceived to have written down assets and have provisions for risks in excess of that allowed or required under IAS or US-GAAP (Breeden [1994]). Bayer reports a "special item with an equity portion" as well as provisions and miscellaneous liabilities totaling more than DM7 billion relative to total assets of around DM40 billion. So, it may seem that Bayer is employing the practice of recording excess provisions. However, once the details of these components were extracted, there were no excessive provisions or material write-downs for tax purposes that were not reversed. To indicate further insights to substantiate this conclusion, some additional details are provided.

The "Special item with an equity component" of DM68 million is a "special" tax deduction, which does not reflect economic substance analogous to an accelerated cost recovery system used for tax purposes in the US. This item is gradually being eliminated. Under IAS and US-GAAP, DM46 million out of

---

2 As of January 1, 1994, the average rate will be used for net income as well.
3 There is no additional adjustment to income because Bayer translates all income components at an average rate.

the DM68 million balance at December 31, 1993 would be allocated to retained earnings and the rest would be added to deferred tax liability. The net adjustment to income would be immaterial.

Of the miscellaneous provisions of DM3.4 billion in 1993, well over DM1 billion had been provided for employee benefits other than pensions. These provisions were all considered to be legitimate accrued expenses. In addition, more than DM500 million had been provided for environmental liabilities. While US companies seem to have been lax in making similar provisions, Bayer's provision seemed quite reasonable given various commitments already in place. The only provision that would not be allowed under IAS or US-GAAP is the accrual for repairs and maintenance to be incurred in the three months following the fiscal year-end. This amount varies little from year to year, so that there is a negligible effect on income, but the provision would be eliminated and shareholders' equity increased by DM21 million (after tax) as a result of this adjustment.

Bayer also reports DM2.9 billion of miscellaneous liabilities. These are actual obligations already incurred for which payment is due. Hence, there is no adjustment for IAS or US-GAAP purposes.

Other operating income and other operating expenses would be largely offset under IAS and US-GAAP. For example, foreign exchange gains are shown under other operating income while foreign exchange losses are shown under other operating expenses. These complementary items are substantial proportions of both categories. As a second example, other operating income includes so-called "sideline revenues." This category includes sales made in the employees' canteens. The cost of this service is reported under "other operating expenses." As this service is run on a break-even basis, the net figure is immaterial yet the grossing-up makes these amounts appear excessive. Consideration of the itemized accounts suggests that no transfers were made that indicated earnings management.

The notes to the financial statements allude to various tax-related write-downs or provisions. In the last two years, all major new write-downs at the legal entity level were reversed prior to consolidation. As of January 1, 1994, such reversal will apply to all tax-related write-downs. Tax-related adjustments in 1993 were immaterial and the tax impact of the remaining balance of DM64 million will be immaterial in any one year. The net effect on shareholders' equity is to increase it by approximately DM32 million.

Minority interests, reported as a component, would be excluded from total shareholders' equity and total net income. A reconciliation of changes in shareholders' equity is required by both IAS and US-GAAP.

D. Property, Plant, and Equipment

Bayer expenses all research and development costs as incurred. This is consistent with US-GAAP but, strictly speaking, some development costs might need to be capitalized under IAS. This amount is not easily quantifiable and would vary from year to year.

The benchmark treatment under IAS is to expense interest while the allowed alternative is capitalization. US-GAAP requires capitalization of borrowing costs, which is a practice not found in Germany presumably because it seems to be at odds with the overriding prudence principle adopted under German law. There is no estimate of what interest might be capitalized for most group companies, but management does not expect it to be material given the nature of the business. Where certain group companies capitalized interest locally, this capitalization was retained for group reporting purposes.

Bayer does not capitalize any noncancelable operating leases, nor does it provide a schedule of payments. However, it discloses the present value of all noncancelable operating leases. Leases totaling DM419 million would qualify for capitalization under IAS and US-GAAP. In 1992, the total would have been around DM330 million. The effect of this practice on the income statement in 1993 was not computed, and it is not cost effective to calculate the adjustment to shareholders' equity given the certain immateriality of any adjustment.

Bayer has no active sale and leaseback arrangements. Besides the obvious understated asset values arising from the use of other historical costs and the tax write-down in prior years of DM53 million not yet reversed, there appear to be no other silent reserves.

E. Investments

Investments in other companies or financial instruments relate primarily to interests in various venture capital companies and in an insurance company. These are expected to be held indefinitely and are valued at the lower of cost and market value.

Marketable securities are recorded at the lower of cost and market value computed on an individual company basis, rather than a portfolio basis as required under US-GAAP. No material adjustment is anticipated for a portfolio-based approach.

Bayer does not provide the disclosures required under SFAS 105 and 107 and as required in the IASC's proposed financial instruments standard (E48). However, Bayer does not engage in any speculative or anticipatory hedges.

F. Discontinued Operations and Changes in Accounting Policies

These items are not separately disclosed under German GAAP in the same manner as IAS or US-GAAP. There were no items in 1993 that would have had any material impact on earnings or shareholders' equity.

G. Taxation

In general, German companies have little need for deferred tax liabilities because of the tax conformity rules (*Maßgeblichkeitsprinzip*) at the legal entity level. Deferred tax assets are usually not recognized because of the prudence principle, although they may be recognized to the extent they offset deferred tax liabilities. In addition, deferred taxes may arise as a result of adjusting entries on consolidation. No deferred tax asset is created for tax loss carryforwards. There is minimal disclosure related to taxes.

A detailed analysis indicated tax loss carryforwards of around DM100 million (primarily in non-German companies) at the end of 1993, but Bayer would probably have created a valuation allowance against the implicit deferred tax asset related to this and so no potential additional asset is considered.

Further, given the lack of material explicit excess provisions or silent reserves in assets, there is little likelihood of any additional deferred taxes beyond those resulting from adjustments already mentioned. However, significant additional disclosures would be required under both IAS and US-GAAP.

H. Post-Employment Benefits

Bayer accrues its pension obligations on the basis of individual country practices. Of the current provision, most applies to the German operations. In German companies, the provision is based on actuarial calculations using existing pay scales and a 6% discount rate as permitted under tax laws. The actuarial calculation was made assuming a higher discount rate and a salary projection. Management had an actuary calculate the pension provision using the approach outlined in IAS 19, which may differ in certain details from US-GAAP on an ongoing basis. The analysis reflected an under-accrual of approximately DM523 million. Under US-GAAP this amount should be accrued over the remaining service life of existing employees, so the adjustment to earnings and shareholders' equity would be approximately DM16 million (after tax) in 1993, assuming adoption in that year.

Because there are no plan assets, for the pensions accrued on the balance sheet the net of service costs and payments made to employees plus interest are accrued each year and included as part of personnel costs. Conceptually, an argument can be made that the interest should be shown as a financial expense rather than as part of operating labor costs, but this is not a requirement under any existing GAAP. Thus, the only additional liability is a result of the change in actuarial assumptions.

As the US operations yield the next-largest part of the pension obligation and of employees as a whole, and as the accrual for any unfunded obligations relating to US employees is based on US-GAAP, no additional accrual is required for these operations. There are no other material defined benefit funds that could have an under- or over-accrual for pensions.

With respect to other post-employment benefits, all health-care-related provisions are made, and accruals are made for early-retirement programs. Given the propensity of German companies to accrue for all possible losses and costs, it is not surprising that the full accrual has been made. However, the disclosures on pension-related costs are virtually nonexistent and are substantially less than required under both IAS and US-GAAP.

I. Revenue Recognition

While German law requires a completed contract basis, Bayer has no significant long-term contracts. Both IAS and US-GAAP require use of a percentage of completion method.

J. Segment Reporting

Bayer presents segment disclosures for sales operating profit and capital expenditures by line-of-business and region. It does not provide segmented information on identifiable assets as required under both IAS and US-GAAP and depreciation by line-of-business required by the latter.

K. Related Party Transactions

No additional disclosures are required.

L. Statement of Cash Flows

German law does not require a statement of cash flows. Bayer presents a funds flow statement, which conforms with the format typically provided by German companies and is a variant of a statement of changes in financial position. It is clearly different from IAS and US-GAAP. Interpretation of the statement provided is not simple. For example, in the financing section, "utilization of long-term provisions" of DM238 million in 1993 actually refers to payments related to the pension provision.

M. Other Items

Bayer includes discount on bonds of DM95 million as a deferred charge. This would be reclassified as a contra liability under both IAS and US-GAAP. Under both IAS and US-GAAP, Bayer would be required to provide additional disclosures of various items. On the other hand, as previously suggested, certain current disclosures would be excluded on the basis of materiality. Also, while management discusses many issues, these would have to be formalized into the management discussion and analysis section required by US regulations. US-GAAP also requires additional information relating to the calculation of earnings per share.

SUMMARY

It is clear from the analysis that if Bayer is typical of German companies, a shift to IAS would move the financial statements substantially towards US-GAAP. Changes in the treatment of foreign currency translation and goodwill are the most material adjustments and these are primarily retroactive in nature. The other changes will largely be a function of reclassification and additional disclosure.

B-3 The Broken Hill Proprietary Company Group

OVERVIEW

The Broken Hill Proprietary Company Ltd. (BHP) is a major international resources company headquartered in Australia with operations in over 20 countries. The most significant operations outside Australia are in New Zealand, the USA, the UK, and South America. BHP is Australia's largest company, contributing approximately 1.5% of Australia's total Gross Domestic Product and more than 8% of total Australian merchandise exports in 1992/93. The group operates in three principal areas of business: minerals exploration and production (principally coal, iron ore, copper concentrate, and manganese ore); hydrocarbon exploration, production, and refining; and steel production. It also operates a significant transportation fleet. BHP's shares (or American Depository Receipts) are listed and traded on the following stock exchanges: Australian, Basel, Frankfurt, Geneva, London, New York, New Zealand, Tokyo, and Zurich. At May 31, 1993, approximately 19.5% of BHP's outstanding shares were held by controlled entities and treated as treasury stock. All other shares were held broadly with no significant or controlling interest.

BHP prepares its principal financial statements under Australian GAAP, an accounting system that has roots in UK and US practices while retaining certain fundamental differences. As BHP has been listed on the New York Stock Exchange since 1987, the detailed data for reconciling to both revised IAS and US-GAAP are available and already audited.[1] Hence, BHP together with Fletcher Challenge provide two illustrations of what information might differ if non-US companies currently registered with the SEC were permitted to use IAS as the benchmark.

---

1 BHP does not provide the supplementary information reflecting the effects of changing prices previously required under IAS 15. However, all other material data required by IAS are provided.

SPECIFIC DIFFERENCES

A. Acquisitions, Business Combinations, and Consolidations

Contrary to IAS and US-GAAP, Australian GAAP precludes companies from using equity accounting in the primary consolidated financial statements, although the information is required to be provided as supplementary information in the notes to the financial statements, as is done by BHP.[2] The impact of equity accounting is to increase equity by A$203 million and earnings by A$80 million in 1993. In general, all other treatments in this category are consistent with both US-GAAP and IAS.

Acquisitions are accounted for as purchases, with the difference between purchase price and the fair value of net assets being capitalized as goodwill and amortized. Australian GAAP specifies that goodwill be amortized over the period of benefit with a maximum period of 20 years. BHP's amortization period is up to 20 years. The company continuously reviews the amount of goodwill to ensure it has not diminished in value; and hence, BHP's practice is consistent with IAS. While BHP does not have material amounts of goodwill or other intangible assets, it is possible under Australian GAAP to capitalize a portion of the acquisition premium to "brand value" or other identifiable intangibles and not amortize this premium, other than to periodically reconsider its value. Currently, the IASC is working on the topic of intangible assets. The existing IAS framework would allow capitalization of an intangible and then would require amortization over the period of benefit. US-GAAP allows for the recognition of intangibles other than goodwill, which should then be amortized over the period of benefit, but not exceeding 40 years.

Under Australian GAAP, negative goodwill is first applied to write down nonmonetary assets and then taken to profit and loss in the year of acquisition. BHP has not had any negative goodwill in excess of the value of the assets and hence has not taken any amounts to earnings, a practice that is incompatible with both IAS and US-GAAP.

BHP uses proportional consolidation for its unincorporated joint ventures. This treatment is considered acceptable under both US-GAAP and IAS because it relates to jointly controlled operations and assets, which are primarily in the natural resources segments. BHP accounts for its associated companies on a cost basis in the consolidated financial statements and on an equity basis in the note.[3]

B. Foreign Currency Translation

Discussions with BHP officials provided details of the company's policy for foreign currency translation. For translation of its foreign subsidiaries, BHP

---

2 Some Australian companies present a multi-column balance sheet and income statement, with and without equity accounting.

3 BHP does not view any of its partly-owned incorporated entities as "joint ventures" under the IAS definitions.

adopts a functional currency approach with the US dollar or local currency as functional currency, consistent with both IAS and US-GAAP. In the case of companies operating under a hyperinflationary environment, BHP uses the US dollar as functional currency. These companies operate in the oil and gas and mining segments with significant exports. All prices are established and invoiced in US dollars, and all surplus funds are kept in US dollars. Hence, BHP's policy is the appropriate choice under both IAS and US-GAAP. Where long-term liabilities are held in a currency other than the Australian dollar and these are "matched" by net assets exposed in the same currency, then the liabilities are considered as a hedge and BHP defers any exchange gains or losses by including them in the exchange fluctuation account (cumulative translation adjustment). This is acceptable under both IAS and US-GAAP.

One difference exists where forward contracts are written for long-term purchases or sales for which there are no "firm commitments" other than generic long-term contracts in some cases. In this situation, BHP defers exchange gains and losses, whereas US-GAAP requires at least part of these exchange differences to be expensed. On revising IAS 21, the IASC excluded the hedging principles contained in the original standard as this practice is to be incorporated into its financial instruments standard. The original IAS 21 and the latest financial instruments exposure draft, E48, would allow BHP to defer the exchange differences. At May 31, 1993, there were no material forward contracts that would require reconciliation.

C. Shareholders' Equity

The note describing shareholders' equity and movements in reserves may appear unusual to a US reader. There are various categories of nondistributable reserves and transfers to and from these reserves that would not exist under US-GAAP and IAS. However, the only issue is one of reclassification. It is difficult to reconstruct a US-GAAP or IAS classification because certain adjustments arising from equity transactions have been taken to the general asset realization and asset revaluation reserves, none of which would exist under US-GAAP; only the last of these would exist under an alternative treatment within IAS. These adjustments relate to the buyback and cancellation of a major parcel of shares.

The general reserve is partly a historical phenomenon whereby BHP charged earnings with depreciation based on the current value of assets. These charges were accumulated and set aside as being nondistributable in order to reflect the increased replacement cost of assets used and hence partially ensure the operating capacity of the entity is maintained before dividends are distributed. This practice is no longer followed. The general reserve is retained earnings from an IAS or US-GAAP perspective. The asset realization and revaluation reserves arise from the upward revaluation of fixed assets (see Sections D and E), a practice that has not occurred for several years. The asset realization reserve can reflect, either by transfer from the revaluation reserve, the revaluation increment on revalued assets when they are sold or otherwise disposed of, or by transfer from profits available for appropriation, the profit on sale of assets (fixed assets or investments).

BHP has an Employee Share Plan, which is equivalent to an ESOP plan in the US. The loans made to the employees to purchase the company's shares have been included as part of receivables in the Australian GAAP statements. US-GAAP requires that this loan be treated as a contra to shareholders' equity. In 1993, this amounts to an A$796 million decrease in shareholders' equity. Under IAS, it is probable that the treatment would be equivalent to US-GAAP based on the Framework. However, there is no specific standard dealing with employee share plans.

A reclassification issue applies to the minority shareholders' interest, which would not form part of shareholders' equity under IAS or US-GAAP. Further, the disclosure of components of minority shareholders' interest is required under Australian GAAP and is not against IAS or US-GAAP.

Two of BHP's subsidiaries issued redeemable preference shares and perpetual preference stock. As Australian GAAP classifies preferred stock as equity, the preference shares have been included as part of minority shareholders' interest. Within each subsidiary, these instruments can probably be classified as equity under both IAS and US-GAAP, although there is some question concerning the redeemable preference shares. However, as they form part of minority interest for the BHP group, any reclassification between debt and equity is unimportant as it would have no impact on the reconciliation to shareholders' equity or earnings.

A further classification issue relates to the treatment of proposed dividends. Under Australian GAAP, proposed dividends are reflected as appropriations once they are proposed, while this appropriation will only occur when they are declared under US-GAAP. The Australian practice is consistent with IAS. In 1993, it appears that no adjustment was required for proposed dividends.

BHP records an adjustment in its US-GAAP reconciliation for a transaction relating to Hamilton Oil. The issue is immaterial, hence it is not addressed specifically.

D. Property, Plant, and Equipment

BHP has from time to time revalued certain property. The last revaluation was made in 1984. The large majority of assets are recorded at historical cost, but as US-GAAP does not permit revaluations, the past revaluations require an adjustment to reduce both shareholders' equity and earnings of A$268 million and A$21 million, respectively. IAS permits revaluations of property, plant, and equipment as an alternative treatment, so the adjustment to earnings or equity would not have been required under IAS. Under the revised IAS, if the alternative treatment of asset revaluations is adopted, then such revaluations must be kept up to date.

As indicated in Section C, BHP has had both asset realization and asset revaluation reserve accounts within shareholders' equity. The former reflects previous revaluation increments that have been realized subsequent to the revaluation and hence would form part of retained earnings under US-GAAP. In the case of BHP, both of these accounts have been written down to a zero balance by an offset of losses on repurchase and cancellation of certain shares. Section C describes the US-GAAP position. Under IAS, the reserve transfers would not have occurred and revaluation of property would have been retained.

A further issue for BHP relates to its treatment of cost capitalization for its oil and gas properties. Historically, the definition of an "area of interest" was considered to be different to a "successful efforts" approach. This difference no longer exists to any material degree, although some residual remains. Consequently, BHP reduces equity by A$83 million and increases earnings by A$28 million in 1993. IAS do not consider industry-specific issues, so there is no position on this item. Similarly, the detailed supplementary oil and gas disclosures required under US-GAAP are not required under IAS.

BHP currently capitalizes interest in a manner consistent with both the allowed alternative of IAS and US-GAAP. Several years ago, BHP did not capitalize interest; consequently, there is a residual adjustment made when conforming to US-GAAP. The adjustment decreased earnings by A$7 million and increased equity by A$15 million in 1993.

The schedules of lease payments aggregates the three- to-five-year payments. While consistent with IAS, these obligations would be shown separately (by year) under US-GAAP.

E. Investments

A small amount of investments, held as a long-term investment, were revalued many years ago. While this treatment is acceptable currently under IAS, revaluation is not allowed under US-GAAP. Consequently, the reversal required by US-GAAP would reduce equity and investments by A$24 million. BHP's disclosure of the fair market value of investments reveals an aggregate value lower than book value. No adjustment is made or required as this is related to the investment in Fosters Brewing, which is an associated company and hence under IAS and US-GAAP would automatically be included on an equity basis. The disclosures of fair values for all investments, and the classification and differential treatments of investments held for varying trading purposes under SFAS 105 and 107, are not considered by IAS although they are under consideration as part of the financial instruments project, E48.

F. Discontinued Operations and Changes in Accounting Policy

Under Australian GAAP, retrospective changes in accounting policy resulting from a statutory requirement or from a new or changed accounting standard are reflected as prior period adjustments to beginning retained earnings, which is consistent with the benchmark treatment of IAS. Under US-GAAP and the IAS alternative, these are shown as cumulative effect adjustments on the face of the income statement, unless the new standard indicates otherwise. BHP had a change in accounting principle in 1993, but its effect was not material.

G. Taxation

The treatment of deferred taxes is consistent with IAS and US-GAAP, although there are additional disclosures required under US-GAAP and the proposed revision of IAS (E49). The effect of tax rate changes is shown as an abnormal item under Australian GAAP, but again this is just a classification issue.

H. Post-Employment Benefits

Under current Australian GAAP, BHP charges its contributions to pension plans to income. Applying an accrual approach required by IAS and US-GAAP leads to an increase in shareholders' equity of A$71 million and a decrease in earnings of A$22 million. There are no material post-employment benefits other than pensions.

With respect to the pension plans, BHP does not provide the disclosures required under US-GAAP or IAS in its annual report. However, this detail is provided in the Form 20-F filed with the SEC.

Australian regulations for pension funds allow industry-based multi-employer plans. Consistent with US-GAAP, these multiemployer plans are treated on a pay-as-you-go basis. IAS 19 does not deal specifically with multi-employer plans.

I. Revenue Recognition

BHP's practices are consistent with IAS and US-GAAP.

J. Segment Reporting

While BHP's Australian GAAP segment disclosures conform to IAS 14, US-GAAP requires additional disclosures of capital expenditure and depreciation by line of business segment. BHP provides this disclosure in its Form 20-F.

K. Related Party Transactions

In conformity with the requirements of Australian GAAP, BHP provides extensive descriptive data about its related party transactions.

L. Statement of Cash Flows

BHP's statement of cash flow is consistent with the requirements of both IAS and US-GAAP.

M. Other Items

Australian income statements report sales plus other revenue and then, as a separate starting point, state "operating profit before depreciation and amortization." The result is that there is no way for a user to obtain cost of goods sold from the data presented. Furthermore, other revenue includes the gross proceeds from sales of noncurrent assets. The net gain on sale of these assets is reported separately in the notes, but the reporting of gross proceeds differs from IAS and US-GAAP.

SUMMARY

BHP's Australian GAAP accounting policies are generally consistent with IAS and US-GAAP. One major difference is the treatment of associated companies; Australian GAAP does not permit the use of equity accounting in the primary consolidated financial statements, although this information is provided in the notes. Aside from these adjustments, the other adjustments are for old revaluations of property and investments (US-GAAP only), use of an accrual basis in pensions, exclusion of minority interests from shareholders' equity, the classification of a loan to an ESOP as a contra-equity, and retroactive adjustments for interest capitalization (US-GAAP only).

B-4 The Cap Gemini Sogeti Group

OVERVIEW

Cap Gemini Sogeti (CGS) is a service company operating in the field of consulting and information technology services. Its primary operations are in France, the United Kingdom, the rest of Europe, and the US. CGS's shares are listed on the Paris Stock Exchange. At the time of this analysis, which is based on the December 31, 1992 annual report, Sogeti S.A., which is personally controlled by the Chairman and Chief Executive Officer of CGS, held 62% of the shares in CGS and controlled more than two-thirds of all voting rights. At that time, Daimler-Benz held 34% of Sogeti's shares so that audited US-GAAP data were available for CGS.[1] CGS prepares its accounts in accordance with French law and the "current statements of accounting practice" issued by the IASC. Consequently, CGS had not yet adopted all aspects of the IASC's improvements project, so some of the differences cited here would disappear once the revised standards are adopted. As a services company, CGS's primary expenses are personnel-related and its largest assets are intangible. Hence, most of the differences from US-GAAP occur in the treatment of intangibles and accounting for business combinations.

SPECIFIC DIFFERENCES

A. Acquisitions, Business Combinations, and Consolidations

Several issues arise within this broad category. Each is considered separately.

---

1 The data had been audited by Daimler-Benz's auditors.

Under IAS 22, the acquisition cost is based on the fair value of the purchase consideration. As no specific mention is made of deferred payments (not based on contingencies) in the original version of IAS 22, CGS recorded the cost of one acquisition at the nominal value of the purchase consideration, although some of the payment was deferred. Under both US-GAAP and revised IAS, such consideration must be recorded at the present value of the purchase consideration. The result of the difference is to increase interest expense and reduce goodwill and short-term debt, with a net reduction in income and shareholders' equity of FF78 million in 1992.

Effective January 1, 1992, CGS increased its stake in one subsidiary so that it changed from an investment to a subsidiary. At that time, the market value of the original investment was less than the book value. CGS had not recognized this difference because it had viewed the true value of the holding to be higher than the market value at the time and so did not write it down, as permitted under IAS 25. This treatment would not have been permitted under US-GAAP. SFAS 12 and SFAS 115 require recognition of the lower value potentially by an adjustment to a shareholders' equity account.

However, under both US-GAAP and revised IAS 22, when the investment becomes part of an acquisition the fair value of the net assets would have to be applied in determining the purchase consideration. Hence, the lower value should be recognized under revised IAS and US-GAAP. CGS did not make this adjustment, which seems to be acceptable under old IAS; this would lead to a reduction of shareholders' equity of FF200 million with an immaterial impact on income in 1992.

For several acquisitions, CGS attributed part of the purchase consideration to an intangible asset classified as "market share," which is not amortized but is reevaluated periodically. While the original IAS 22 permits this treatment, revised IAS 22 and US-GAAP do not. Consequently, an adjustment would be made transferring the "market share" to "goodwill" and then accruing amortization expenses from the relevant acquisition dates. The market share elimination will not affect shareholders' equity except to the extent of the goodwill amortization. For a 40-year amortization period used in 1992, the reduction of income and shareholders' equity would have been approximately FF85 million. There is also an adjustment to minority interest for their portion of the capitalized "market share."

CGS has adopted a 40-year period for amortizing goodwill, which is permissible under the original IAS 22 and arguably under US-GAAP. However, given the nature of the business, the SEC is likely to push for a much shorter life with a likely maximum of 15 years. Under revised IAS 22, a firm should look to the economic life with an expected 5-year amortization period unless a longer life can be justified. But there is now a maximum amortization period of 20 years. Hence, under both revised IAS and SEC-guided US-GAAP, CGS would have to significantly reduce its goodwill (including market share) and increase the rate of amortization. Revised IAS does not require retroactive adjustment, but it does require an annual reevaluation of the goodwill. It can be assumed that a shift to a 20-year amortization would be made, which would reduce shareholders' equity by approximately FF400 million with a reduction in 1992 income of approximately FF150 million.

In 1992, CGS entered into a joint venture and accounted for its investment using proportional consolidation. The proportional method is the benchmark treatment under IAS 31, but under US-GAAP only the equity method is permitted. While this has no direct effect on shareholders' equity or earnings, each component reported separately would be affected. The two components likely to be impacted the most are sales and goodwill. Since the time of the 1992 annual report, the SEC has allowed non-US companies to use proportional consolidation.

In 1992, a provision for restructuring costs was created, a significant portion of which related to two acquisitions. The auditors are satisfied that the provision is in conformity with IAS and French GAAP. Extensive audit analysis revealed that the accruals were materially consistent with US-GAAP, so no adjustment was anticipated.

Many French companies reflect the goodwill implicit in the investment in associate companies separately, as part of the goodwill of the group rather than as part of the investment account. This treatment differs from IAS and US-GAAP but would only lead to a reclassification without any explicit adjustment to shareholders' equity or income.

IAS 22 (original and revised) and US-GAAP require disclosure of the purchase consideration for acquisitions. This information was not provided by CGS although, given the nature of the business, it can be largely inferred from the goodwill data disclosed.

Some subsidiaries are not consolidated. CGS asserted that these were immaterial in all respects and so would have no impact on any US-GAAP statements.

B. Foreign Currency Translation

CGS's practices are consistent with IAS and US-GAAP. There would need to be a statement on accounting policies for foreign currency transactions.

C. Shareholders' Equity

An accrual for the possible risk of having to pay a premium on redemption of convertible bonds was made in 1992. Under US-GAAP and E48, the premium would be accrued over the life of the bond. The effect on shareholders' equity is immaterial and the effect on income was an increase of approximately FF20 million in 1992.

In 1987 through 1992, stock options were issued to employees at between 80% and 90% of the market value at the time. This discount should be reflected as compensation expense under US-GAAP. The impact on income in 1992 would have been immaterial at approximately FF5 million. The shareholders' equity would have no material impact other than from reclassification, which has no effect in a US-GAAP reconciliation.

In 1986, debenture loans with equity warrants were issued. This analysis does not take up the question as to whether some amount of value would be attached to these warrants, as by 1992 any material adjustment would be a reclassification within shareholders' equity and irrelevant to a reconciliation.

D. Property, Plant, and Equipment

As a service company, CGS has relatively little property, plant, and equipment. It does have (uncapitalized) noncancelable operating leases, for which both IAS and US-GAAP require additional disclosure with respect to the payment schedule.

Further, while some software is capitalized, most research and development is expensed. The capitalized software should probably be expensed both in terms of IAS and US-GAAP. The impact is on intangible assets current income, minority interest, and shareholders' equity. At the end of 1992, the impact on shareholders' equity was a reduction of FF12 million with an immaterial impact on income.

E. Investments

Similar to the situation described in Section A, CGS has a 28% stake in a company that is not reported under the equity method because a competitor to CGS has a controlling interest; CGS deems it has no significant influence as it does not even have a representative on the company's Board of Directors. It is likely that use of the cost method could be retained under IAS and US-GAAP. The 1992 Annual Report discloses that the cost of this investment is higher than the market value by FF153 million (after tax), which CGS chooses not to adjust as it views it to be a long-term investment with long-term value. Under US-GAAP, the investment would be written down and a contra-equity account created with no income effect.

Based on current US-GAAP and proposed IAS, CGS will be required to expand its disclosure on its investments in financial instruments in the future.

F. Discontinued Operations and Changes in Accounting Policies

No such items arose in 1992 for CGS. However, CGS's classification of exceptional items would not be classified as such under IAS or US-GAAP. See also Section K.

G. Taxation

Deferred taxes are treated consistently with IAS and US-GAAP at the time of the financial statements. The disclosures are also largely provided in conformity with US-GAAP; the one apparent difference is a split between domestic and foreign portions. Under SFAS 109 and proposed IAS (E49), one can expect to see additional disclosures and perhaps a higher deferred tax asset related to the deferred tax loss carryforwards. However, the subjective nature of the valuation allowance makes this value difficult to compute.

H. Post-Employment Benefits

Where defined benefit pension plans exist, they are unfunded and accrued based on projected salary levels. There appear to be no other post-employment benefits offered. While the disclosure on pensions is not as detailed as under revised IAS and US-GAAP, the materiality and complexity of the pension obligations is much less for CGS than for an equivalent US company. No adjustment was considered necessary to comply with US-GAAP, although this was not fully audited.

I. Revenue Recognition

CGS uses a percentage of completion method as required by IAS and US-GAAP. One would expect to see more disclosure about the various cost and payments components under both sets of standards.

J. Segment Reporting

CGS has only one line of business but reports four geographic segments for sales. This segment disclosure is more limited than required under IAS or US-GAAP standards, which require segment disclosures of operating income and assets in addition to sales.

K. Related Party Transactions

CGS has had extensive related party transactions, including the sale of various assets to related parties. For example, in 1992 CGS reported a gain of FF318 million (pretax) from the sale of a building to its holding company, and in 1991 a gain of FF129 million (pretax) on the sale of shares in one company to an associate company also controlled by CGS's parent. It is likely that under revised IAS and as required under US-GAAP these gains (or a portion thereof) would have to be reversed. As the transactions were made at fair market values, no adjustments are made to shareholders' equity, although these items would be subject to closer scrutiny during a formal registration process, to ensure appropriate classification.

L. Statement of Cash Flows

The statement of cash flows is largely in conformity with revised IAS 7 and US-GAAP. The additional disclosures required include the cash amounts paid for tax and interest.

M. Other Items

In 1991, CGS made a payment to a third party that was given the irrevocable responsibility of servicing some debt. CGS accounted for this transaction as an in-substance defeasance, but it would not qualify under US-GAAP (nor under proposed IAS in E48) for such a treatment. Hence, the debt and investment would be shown on the balance sheet and the gain recognized in 1991 amortized over the remaining life of the debt via the relative net interest effect. The 1991 pretax income statement effect was FF34.6 million in 1991. Thus, 1991 income and 1992 shareholders' equity would be reduced by the net of tax amount less the amortization of the balance of approximately FF20 million.

Many items normally discussed in the management discussion and analysis section are discussed by CGS in various parts of its report. This would be summarized and enhanced under SEC guidelines.

SUMMARY

CGS follows IAS prior to revisions under the improvements project. The major areas of adjustment relate to acquisitions and sales of significant equity stakes in companies with which it is affiliated. In particular, the asset "market share" would be classified as goodwill and amortized; we would also find additional disclosures in several areas, notably segment reporting of income and assets on a geographical basis.

B-5 The Fletcher Challenge Group

OVERVIEW

Fletcher Challenge (FC) is one of the largest companies based in New Zealand with significant operations in several other countries, including Australia, North and South America, the United Kingdom, and the Pacific Basin. Group companies operate in pulp and paper products, building material and construction, agricultural servicing, and energy sectors. The company's shares were listed on the New Zealand, Australian, London, and three Canadian stock exchanges in August 1993. Subsequently, the group has listed its shares on the New York Stock Exchange. At August 1993, besides the Employee Unit Trust and other employee funds (21%), the two largest direct shareholders were the Australian Mutual Provident Society (7.6%) and the Queen in Right of New Zealand (6.7%).

Over the last five years, and especially in its 1992 fiscal year, FC adjusted several of its accounting policies to conform with both IAS and US-GAAP where permitted under New Zealand rules. Consequently, most of the potential adjustments that might exist under a "traditional" New Zealand approach are not required for FC. Further, as FC is currently listed on the New York Stock Exchange, the detailed data for reconciling to both IAS and US-GAAP are available. Hence, together with BHP, FC provides some insight as to how a current SEC-registrant might be impacted by the application of IAS versus US-GAAP. The June 30, 1993 annual financial statements were used for this analysis. These statements went beyond New Zealand-GAAP [NZ-GAAP] requirements in several instances.

SPECIFIC DIFFERENCES

A. Acquisitions, Business Combinations, and Consolidations

In general, the treatment is consistent with both US-GAAP and IAS. Acquisitions are accounted for as purchases, with the difference between purchase price and the fair value of net assets being capitalized as goodwill and amortized.

FC's amortization period is stated as being generally "five years or less; however, in individual cases may be up to twenty years." The cases in which goodwill is amortized in less than five years are apparently immaterial. The benchmark of 5 years with a 20-year maximum is consistent with IAS and US-GAAP as it is based on expected useful life.

FC's accounting policies note a treatment for negative goodwill in which the amount is first applied to write down nonmonetary assets and then "taken to Earnings." The application of negative goodwill to write down assets was one of the changes made by FC in 1992 to facilitate conformity to IAS and US-GAAP. In recent times there has not been any balance remaining after the write down of assets, so a potential adjustment that would have arisen if negative goodwill had been taken to earnings is not required.

One difference from US-GAAP identified by FC relates to the treatment of deferred tax assets on acquisition. Under NZ-GAAP, deferred taxes are not adjusted for the value of unutilized tax loss carryforwards. Under current US-GAAP, such a deferred tax asset would be recognized as part of the purchase consideration. While the current US-GAAP is consistent with IAS, it is not required under IAS. The adjustment is to reduce earnings by NZ$5.4 million and to reduce shareholders' equity by NZ$59.7 million.

FC uses proportional consolidation for its joint ventures. These are in the oil and gas sector and hence this treatment is considered acceptable under US-GAAP as well as complying with the benchmark treatment of IAS. Furthermore, the SEC currently permits non-US registrants to use proportional consolidation. Therefore, no adjustment is required.

B. Foreign Currency Translation

For translation of its foreign subsidiaries, FC adopts a functional currency approach consistent with both IAS and US-GAAP. In the case of companies operating in a hyperinflationary economy, FC uses the US dollar as functional currency. As these companies operate in the oil and gas and forestry segments, which have prices established in US dollars, it is believed that this is the correct choice under both sets of GAAP.

One difference that exists is that FC uses the year-end rate to translate its income statement and cash flow items in accordance with NZ-GAAP. The company indicates in its report that there is no material effect on earnings in 1993; the company further states that the cumulative effect, which might lead to a reclassification between retained earnings and the cumulative translation adjustment, is also immaterial. However, in principle, this treatment differs both from revised IAS 21 and US-GAAP.[1]

---

1 In the original exposure draft amending IAS 21 as part of the improvements project, the IASC permitted use of the closing rate for the income statement. The author believes that, from a shareholders' value perspective, this treatment is logically more consistent than either US-GAAP or the revised version of IAS 21.

Another treatment that may differ from both US-GAAP and IAS is with respect to anticipated hedges. Under NZ-GAAP, a company can hedge foreign currency exposure on anticipated transactions and amortize any deferral over 12 months. FC appears to no longer utilize this practice as there is no reconciling item in 1993, but it still indicates the practice under its accounting policy statements.

A final issue with foreign currency translation relates to the treatment of hedged foreign currency liabilities. FC's accounting policy states that "Foreign currency liabilities subject to a forward exchange hedge contract are recorded at the contract rate." This would cause a difference if the maturity of the contracts differed from the loan, but FC stated that this does not occur. The policy would also apply to assets if they existed.

C. Shareholders' Equity

The note describing shareholders' equity and movements in reserves may appear unusual to a US reader. There are various categories of nondistributable reserves and transfers to and from these reserves, which would not exist under US-GAAP and IAS. However, the only issue is one of reclassification with the share premium, capital redemption, general capital, and capital replacement reserves all being part of additional paid-in capital; the rest is part of retained earnings or cumulative translation adjustment.

Shareholders' equity is reduced by various amounts relating to the Employee Unit Trust and Employee Share Purchase Scheme. These appear to be equivalent to ESOP plans in the US and hence the treatment appears to be consistent with US-GAAP. No IAS exists for this topic.

A reclassification issue applies to the minority shareholders' interest, which would not form part of shareholders' equity under IAS or US-GAAP. No explicit adjustment is required as FC has a separate sum for group equity without the minority interest. Further, the disclosure of components of minority shareholders' interest required under NZ-GAAP is not against IAS or US-GAAP.

A further classification issue relates to the treatment of proposed dividends. Under NZ-GAAP, proposed dividends are reflected as appropriations once they are proposed, while this appropriation will only occur when dividends are declared (i.e., approved by shareholders) under US-GAAP. The NZ-GAAP treatment is permitted by IAS. Under US-GAAP, the shareholders' equity would increase by NZ\$86.1 million as a result of this change.

FC has various instruments it has used to raise capital, which are of the form of "Capital Notes" and "Exchangeable Perpetual Preference Shares." These have been structured so that the holders bear equity risk and are therefore classified as part of equity rather than as debt. It is apparent that these instruments can be classified as equity under both IAS based on the Framework and E48 and current US-GAAP.

D. Property, Plant, and Equipment

FC's practices largely conform to IAS and US-GAAP. One change FC made in order to move closer to IAS and US-GAAP was to eliminate its revaluation of certain property. This change was made in 1992 with no residual adjustment required. Hence, while FC's practice conforms to US-GAAP, many NZ firms might have revalued assets; this would necessitate adjustment when conforming to US-GAAP, but not for IAS purposes.

One disclosure difference is that capitalized leased assets are reported at their book value rather than shown at cost and accumulated depreciation as required by IAS and US-GAAP. Further, while no separate schedule of payments for these leased assets is provided, the future payments are included in the schedule provided for all long-term obligations.

The notes to the accounts also discuss a special depreciation charge to write down assets under certain circumstances. FC stated that this relates solely to permanent impairment situations, which is thus consistent with both IAS and US-GAAP.

E. Investments

FC provides extensive disclosures consistent with current requirements of US-GAAP and proposed IAS based on E48.

F. Discontinued Operations and Changes in Accounting Policy

Under NZ-GAAP and the benchmark treatment of IAS, changes in accounting policies are reflected as prior period adjustments to beginning retained earnings. Under US-GAAP and the IAS alternative, these are shown as cumulative effect adjustments on the face of the income statement. In 1993, this difference would have reduced NZ-GAAP income by NZ$86.3 million to conform to US-GAAP.

Similarly, the sale of a segment of the business is classified as an abnormal item under NZ-GAAP, while under IAS and US-GAAP this would be shown as a separate line item after operating income. This is a reclassification issue only and amounted to NZ$44.1 million in 1993.

G. Taxation

The treatment of deferred taxes is consistent with IAS and US-GAAP, although there are some additional disclosures required under US-GAAP and the proposed revision to IAS (E49).

The tax loss carryforwards are treated as deferred tax assets after a valuation allowance and are considered to be treated consistently with US-GAAP and IAS, subject to the adjustment discussed in Section A.

H. Post-Employment Benefits

FC indicates that it changed its accounting policy in 1993 to accrue for "nonpension related post-retirement benefit costs." This applies to health care; there are no other post-employment benefits other than pensions. Thus, all measures are consistent with both IAS and US-GAAP.

With respect to the pension plans, there are disclosures required under US-GAAP that would also cover IAS. However, there is no detail provided in the annual report on the non-pension benefits for which the change was made in 1993. Nonetheless, the disclosures do conform to the requirements in force at that time.

I. Revenue Recognition

FC's practices are consistent with IAS and US-GAAP.

J. Segment Reporting

FC provides detailed segment disclosures. Under US-GAAP, additional line of business disclosures of depreciation and capital expenditures are required.

K. Related Party Transactions

FC provides a detailed discussion of transactions with related parties.

L. Statement of Cash Flows

FC provides a cash flow statement, which is consistent with IAS and US-GAAP.

M. Other Items

FC provides significant disclosures relating to their energy and forestry businesses, as required under US-GAAP. IAS is silent on industry-specific items other than for general requirements in the Framework.

SUMMARY

FC has few differences from either IAS or US-GAAP, but this is in part because it has chosen to move its policies to these criteria where permitted by NZ-GAAP. The analysis reveals some differences between the benchmark IAS and US-GAAP, particularly in accounting for joint ventures, treatment of changes in accounting policies, and accounting for acquired deferred tax assets. In all three cases, IAS and NZ-GAAP are consistent. While the measurement differences are slight, there are several additional disclosures provided to conform with US-GAAP that may not have been provided under current NZ-GAAP or IAS.

B-6 The Holderbank Group

OVERVIEW

The Holderbank Group of companies operates in the cement and related building products industries. The group has its headquarters in Switzerland and has major operating subsidiaries in Europe, North America, Latin America, South Africa, and Australia. It also has investments in other countries, with increasing investments in Asia. The holding company's shares are traded on the three Swiss stock exchanges and on SEAQ International in London. Many of the subsidiaries are public companies listed on their own local exchanges. Mr. Thomas Schmidheiny is the Chairman of the Board of Directors and the Executive Committee and is the largest single shareholder.

The group has a decentralized management approach with a small controlling and group reporting staff in Switzerland. The whole group adopted IAS as the required basis from January 1, 1992. Each of the group companies was required to adopt IAS simultaneously, with a group reporting package developed to ensure that the group standards are applied. The analysis presumes all companies in the group apply group accounting policies consistently.

As this analysis was prepared on the basis of the 1992 annual report, the revisions to the IAS from the IASC's improvements project had not been completed. Nevertheless, the IAS adopted by Holderbank were based on the presumed implementation of the exposure drafts from the improvements project, so there have been some changes in accounting policy as the exposure drafts were amended prior to full adoption. Where the IAS still allows alternative policies, Holderbank has made explicit choices, generally using the benchmark treatment. In 1993, Holderbank used the policies in the revised standards, which are used as the basis of comparison in this analysis.

Holderbank is not a Coopers & Lybrand client but is audited by another international audit firm.

SPECIFIC DIFFERENCES

A. Acquisitions, Business Combinations, and Consolidations

Prior to introducing IAS, on acquisition of a majority share in a company, Holderbank would adjust the net assets to a fair value and then eliminate the difference directly against retained earnings. As of January 1, 1992, the policy was changed to capitalize the goodwill and amortize it over an expected useful life. The amortization periods consider the nature of the operations in estimating an expected useful life, which varies from 5 to 20 years. However, as allowed under the revised IAS, no retroactive adjustment was made. US-GAAP requires retroactive adjustment. Considering all material acquisitions made throughout the group from 1972 onwards, the total adjustment to US-GAAP would be an increase of shareholders' equity of SFr213 million and a decrease in earnings of SFr8 million.

A second issue relates to the treatment of a French company in which there is an indirect agreement of control, although in 1992 there was no direct or indirect control, despite the fact that the process was underway to formalize control at that time. Holderbank has fully consolidated the company, which would probably not be acceptable under a strict application of IAS or US-GAAP. There is no direct impact on the earnings in 1992, although an adjustment reducing shareholders' equity by SFr49 million was required. In addition, several of the component accounts would be affected. Majority ownership is anticipated to be held by the end of 1994.

A related matter is the accounting treatment for joint ventures. In compliance with the benchmark treatment of IAS 31, Holderbank has adopted the proportional consolidation approach. At the time of the 1992 annual report, US-GAAP required the equity method to be applied to all associated companies. Again, there is no effect on earnings or shareholders' equity, but the individual line items of the statements would have been affected. For example, sales would have been reduced by approximately SFr827 million. However, the SEC currently allows non-US registrants to apply proportional consolidation with summary information about such operations provided on a supplementary basis.

B. Foreign Currency Translation

With the introduction of IAS principles, Holderbank adjusted its foreign currency translation policy to a local currency as functional currency approach for all subsidiaries other than those operating in hyperinflationary countries. In the latter cases, which are primarily the subsidiaries in Latin America, the group uses the US dollar as functional currency. All local accounts and performance evaluations are based on the US dollar accounts, so it is the operational currency. However, the sales are invoiced in local currencies. The SEC has generally taken the position that for non-US companies the functional currency of subsidiaries operating in hyperinflationary economies is the reporting currency of the parent, which must be used if the sales are invoiced in local currency. It is difficult, however, to support the SEC's position on an economic basis if the operating currency in a hyperinflationary country is a reserve currency, as is the case for the US dollar in many Latin American countries, especially if that currency is the basis of operating decisions.

Holderbank's treatment is consistent with IAS. The adjustment required if Holderbank were to apply the SEC position of having the Swiss Franc as the functional currency is not calculable without extraordinary expense, which is unjustifiable.[1] In December 1994, the SEC has accepted the IAS 21 treatment for subsidiaries operating in hyperinflationary economies for non-US registrants. But it is too soon to tell whether this new policy will apply to the choice of the functional currency.

C. Shareholders' Equity

Holderbank considers minority shareholders' interest as part of total shareholders' equity and discloses Holderbank's share as a separate component within shareholders' equity. Under IAS and US-GAAP, minority shareholders' interest is considered as a separate component. From an investor's perspective this is a pure reclassification item, although it is often found on summary reconciliations to US-GAAP.

D. Property, Plant, and Equipment

Holderbank capitalizes certain leased assets using the guidelines under IAS 17 and discloses future payment obligations for both finance (capital) and operating leases in a form equivalent to US-GAAP. Therefore, all capital leases under US-GAAP are treated as such.

E. Investments

Holderbank defines cash equivalents to include investments that mature within 12 months of the fiscal year-end, which is consistent with IAS 13, although 3 months would be used under US-GAAP, implying that a reclassification would be required. Furthermore, the short-term marketable securities are all valued at market values while US-GAAP was based on a lower of cost or market principle at year-end 1992. Holderbank's policy was based on the IASC's exposure

---

1 To the extent that purchasing power parity holds between the US dollar and the local currency in the hyperinflationary economy, as is usual over time in such economies, the difference between the Holderbank and SEC approaches would be the US dollar-Swiss Franc changes over time. As this "value" would be unavailable to a Swiss shareholder, it is suggested that the SEC approach is not economically relevant.

draft on financial instruments E40 (replaced by E48). Market value information and use of fair value for investments held for sale has become required
under US-GAAP and may become required under IAS. Thus, Holderbank was
anticipating the evolving practice. Furthermore, excluding the market value
adjustment to return to the original cost at the 1992 balance sheet date would
have been immaterial, so no adjustment would have been required.

F. Discontinued Operations and Changes in Accounting Policy

As indicated, in 1992 Holderbank changed many of its accounting policies in
moving to IAS. As permitted by the IASC, adoption of the revised IAS did not
require retroactive adjustment for the revised accounting policies. US-GAAP
requires retroactive adjustment with the cumulative effect reflected separately.
The US-GAAP adjustments are reported separately within each category.

There were no discontinued operations for Holderbank.

G. Taxation

Holderbank's policy is to provide for deferred taxation using the liability method
and the partial approach, which was originally accepted as an alternative practice by the IASC as part of its proposed revision of IAS 12 (*IASC Insight*, June
1993). In the current proposed revised standard (E49), the partial method will
no longer be an option. In that case, Holderbank will be required to adopt the
US-GAAP equivalent comprehensive approach. The impact of the difference is
already disclosed in the notes to the financial statements. In 1992, earnings
would be SFr35 million lower and the deferred tax liability would be SFr388
million higher, although only SFr225 million would relate to Holderbank's shareholders.

A second issue that arises is the treatment of deferred tax assets. SFAS 109
has reversed SFAS 96 and allows deferred tax assets to be recognized under less
restrictive conditions. In those subsidiaries with net timing differences that
would lead to deferred tax assets, a detailed analysis of all potential deferred
tax assets and liabilities was compiled by the company. The only material item
that could lead to a deferred tax asset was net operating loss carryforwards,
some of which are recognized. The unrecognized portion would probably be
offset by a valuation allowance under US-GAAP.

The final issue under taxation relates to disclosure. Both IAS and US-GAAP
were undergoing changes at the time of the 1992 annual report. One disclosure
required under US-GAAP even at that time was the reconciliation of the statutory rate to the effective tax rate. The nature of the Swiss taxation system, in
which there is no equivalent to the US federal statutory rate, makes this disclosure close to impossible and certainly meaningless. Given the approach of taxing
the legal entity and not the worldwide group, the statutory rate of the holding
company is not a good indicator of the group's statutory rate. Holderbank

reports a reconciliation to the effective tax rate based on an expected tax expense, and it is plausible that this would be acceptable as reasonable disclosure for US-GAAP purposes. From an investor's perspective, it seems reasonable to conclude that an attempt to comply with a narrow interpretation of the disclosure requirement would be of little incremental benefit. Under SFAS 109, additional disclosures of the differences between the accounting and tax bases of assets and liabilities would be required.

H. Post-Employment Benefits

For pensions, most Holderbank group companies have defined contribution plans that are funded on an annual basis. The only affiliates that have material defined benefit plans are the North American companies (which already comply with US-GAAP), the South African companies, and the German subsidiaries. Each of these companies accrues obligations under defined benefit pension plans in accordance with revised IAS and US-GAAP. The German companies completed this change in 1993, so that the 1992 accounts require an adjustment to shareholders' equity of approximately SFr20 million.

For other post-employment benefits, material employee health care benefits exist only in the US, and SFAS 106 requirements for the North American group are already considered in the 1992 financial statements. Thus, Holderbank's accruals are materially consistent with both IAS and US-GAAP. Similarly, group companies are required to accrue for any post-employment benefits relating to any structural changes (e.g., restructuring). Hence, no additional accruals would have occurred had SFAS 112 been operative at that time. Additional disclosures of the pension cost would be required under US-GAAP.

I. Revenue Recognition

Holderbank's practices are consistent with IAS and US-GAAP.

J. Segment Reporting

The 1992 annual report contains line-of-business segment disclosures that, except for missing data on depreciation, are consistent with US-GAAP. However, it does not provide geographical segment data. Such disclosures are required by both IAS and US-GAAP. Holderbank reports sales and operating income by geographical segment in its 1993 report.

K. Related Party Transactions

As a result of the large holdings of Mr. Thomas Schmidheiny and his other industrial interests, the potential exists in any year for related party transactions. Holderbank discloses this information in a footnote in the 1992 annual report and anticipates providing full disclosure in the future, as appropriate.

There is some uncertainty as to whether each subsidiary has disclosed any related party transactions specific to its own group. But the group intends accessing this information for future purposes and it is arguably required under IAS 24 as well as under US-GAAP.

L. Statement of Cash Flows

Except for the use of a 12-month cut-off for cash equivalents, as indicated in Section E, Holderbank provides a cash flow statement in conformity with IAS 7, which is equivalent to and accepted for US-GAAP purposes.

M. Other Items

Certain items in the income and cash flow statements could be reclassified. For example, the item labeled "extraordinary income" is really "unusual income." As the item was not treated as extraordinary for calculation of net earnings or earnings per share, it has no other impact. The earnings per share data would normally be disclosed on the income statement, while they are shown in a note by Holderbank.

Some items on the cash flow statement could be aggregated. In several notes, reference is made to immaterial items that would normally be ignored under IAS and US-GAAP. An example can be found in the inventory note. In other notes, elaboration of the disclosures would make the meaning clearer to investors. The SEC may require such additional information in certain cases, for example, with respect to the discussion of contingencies and environmental liabilities. The management discussion and analysis section required by the SEC is largely incorporated in the narrative preceding Holderbank's financial statements.

SUMMARY

With the shift to IAS in 1992, Holderbank's financial statements comply with IAS, including the anticipated revisions at the time of the financial statements, except for disclosure of geographic segment income. In most cases, this was also consistent with the measurement requirements of US-GAAP. The primary exceptions are retroactive application of the treatment of acquired goodwill and use of the comprehensive versus partial method of deferred tax accrual.

B-7 The Olivetti Group

OVERVIEW

Olivetti is an Italian-based multinational corporation operating in the field of technology concentrating in the areas of systems, products, and services. The group operates in Italy and most parts of Europe. It also has operations in several other countries outside Europe. Olivetti's common stock is listed in Italy on the Milan Stock Exchange and the Chairman and Chief Executive Officer is the largest single shareholder.

Listed companies in Italy utilize International Accounting Standards where the Italian law and accounting principles are silent, at least with respect to measurement issues. Olivetti follows this practice, so its policies are essentially consistent with IAS. The annual report at December 31, 1992 is used in this analysis; consequently, Olivetti had not yet incorporated revised IAS or the new Italian accounting legislation incorporating the Fourth and Seventh Directives of the European Community. This new legislation will be adopted for the first time in the 1994 financial statements.

AT&T had a 25% stake in Olivetti through fiscal year-end 1989. Consequently, Olivetti had audited reconciliations to US-GAAP through that time.[1] Where feasible, these are used as a basis for the reconciliations provided. Consequently, while the final reconciling items have not been audited at December 31, 1992, the material components have been.

SPECIFIC DIFFERENCES

A. Acquisitions, Business Combinations, and Consolidations

Olivetti measures goodwill arising on acquisitions based on the fair value of net assets acquired. But the company chooses to write off the goodwill against

---

[1] The US-GAAP adjustments had been audited by Olivetti's previous auditors, Arthur Andersen & Co., not by Coopers & Lybrand L.L.P.

shareholders' equity in the year of acquisition. This is consistent with IAS prior to the revision IAS 22, but is inconsistent with US-GAAP, the revised IAS, and the most recent Italian accounting law. Olivetti will adjust its treatment of goodwill by 1994. Olivetti will not need to make any retroactive adjustment for IAS, but such an adjustment would be required under US-GAAP.

Based on the nature of Olivetti's business, it chose to use a 5- to 10-year life even when applying US-GAAP (for AT&T). Using the five-year-life benchmark treatment of IAS 22, which is consistent with US-GAAP, the impact on net income in 1992 would be a decrease (increased loss) of Lira 80 billion and an increase in shareholders' equity of Lira 100 billion. If a ten-year life were to be used, the impact on net income in 1992 would be a decrease (increased loss) of Lira 60 billion and an increase in shareholders' equity of Lira 300 billion.

A second difference from US-GAAP and revised IAS arises because not all subsidiaries are consolidated. Both management and the auditors made assurances that their inclusion would have no material impact on any component of the balance sheet or income statement. Furthermore, at the time of the US-GAAP adjustments for AT&T, no adjustment for unconsolidated subsidiaries occurred.

B. Foreign Currency Translation

Olivetti uses the principles in IAS 21 to translate its subsidiaries operating in hyperinflationary economies. Thus, it price-level-adjusts the local currency accounts and then translates the adjusted accounts at the current rate. The SEC has adopted a stance that if the subsidiary invoices in local currency, then the parent currency should be the functional currency for subsidiaries operating in hyperinflationary economies. This treatment would require measurement of local currency amounts into Italian Lira. However, either the practice applied by Olivetti or use of the US dollar as functional currency is more consistent with economic substance. In December 1994, the treatment used by Olivetti for its subsidiaries operating in hyperinflationary environments was accepted by the SEC for non-US registrants. The impact on the accounts was not quantifiable at year-end 1992. In 1989, a US-GAAP approach based on the Lira as functional currency resulted in a Lira 8 billion (pretax) increase in income and a Lira 92 billion reduction in shareholders' equity.

In 1992, the European Monetary System collapsed and, in September of that year, the Italian Lira experienced a steep devaluation. Under previous and revised IAS 21, the resulting foreign currency losses on purchases can be capitalized. Olivetti accounted for such losses arising in the last four months of the year as part of production costs. It is likely that some, if not most, of the capitalized amount of Lira 10 billion (pretax) would be expensed under US-GAAP.

C. Shareholders' Equity

Costs of capital increases are deferred and amortized by Olivetti, but would be written off against the equity at issuance under US-GAAP. In 1992, the impact would be to increase net income by approximately Lira 3 billion and reduce shareholders' equity by Lira 3 billion.

Historically, Olivetti issued employee stock options below market value without recognizing any compensation expense. This was not a problem in 1992. In 1989, the impact was to reduce net income by Lira 4 billion, so no material adjustments are expected in 1992.

Olivetti has issued bonds with detachable warrants at interest rates below market rates for similar instruments without warrants. Olivetti did not attach any value to these warrants, whereas US-GAAP and proposed IAS (E48) requires that a value be assigned to these warrants and treated as shareholders' equity and netted against the obligation. This amount is then amortized over the life of the bond. At year-end 1992, the balance will require increase in shareholders' equity of Lira 180 billion (after tax).

D. Property, Plant, and Equipment

Italian law has permitted or required revaluations of assets from time to time. The revaluations increase the value of the assets and create a reserve that does not flow through income, but is added to equity. The asset is then depreciated using the new base and the extra depreciation becomes tax deductible. The revaluation reserve is retained separately, even if the assets are fully used up or disposed of. The 1991 revaluation incurred a flat 16 percent tax. The balance of revaluation reserves is taxable only if it is distributed to shareholders. However, the reserves can be used within the revaluing entity to offset losses incurred and never incur tax. In a similar manner, gains recorded by the parent company, arising from organization changes, and eliminated on consolidation, were partially utilized in 1992 to cover some 1991 losses.

Since 1989, the revaluation reserves have increased primarily as a result of the 1991 revaluation amounting to Lira 86 billion. In 1989, the reconciliation to US-GAAP accounted for an increase in income of Lira 24 billion and a decrease in shareholders' equity of Lira 238 billion. Assuming an equivalent rate of amortization (on the gross reserve) and accounting for other changes, a conservative estimate of the adjustments are depreciation expense down (income up), by Lira 30 billion, and shareholders' equity down by Lira 240 billion.

The company provides disclosure of lease commitments in three periods rather than the six periods required under US-GAAP. Most of the leasing business is no longer handled by group companies, so there is unlikely to be any adjustment for capitalization of leases despite a small adjustment made in 1989 at the time of the US-GAAP adjustment for AT&T.

E. Investments

Olivetti employs a lower of cost or market value rule for its financial instruments, applied on a portfolio basis. However, it makes this evaluation based on portfolios defined by the type of instrument (e.g., fixed income versus equity) rather than the classifications required under SFAS 115. While the data are not available, it is conceivable that there may be a difference to US-GAAP as a result of any reclassification of the portfolios, although it is unlikely to be material. Disclosure is provided of the amount that aggregate market value of quoted investments exceeds the carrying cost (Lira 11 billion) and of the fiscal year-end commitments related to various financial instruments. These treatments are believed to be consistent with the requirements of US-GAAP and IAS (including E48). As disclosure standards evolve in the area of financial instruments, additional disclosures can be expected.

In 1992, Olivetti recognized a gain of Lira 55 billion as a result of a counterparty exercising an option that was part of an interest rate swap. IAS and US-GAAP are still evolving in the way they deal with hedged transactions. Consequently, adjustments have not been made, although at the time of the 1992 annual report the Lira 55 billion may have been deferred under US-GAAP.

F. Discontinued Operations and Changes in Accounting Policies

Olivetti's practices are consistent with IAS and US-GAAP.

G. Taxation

There are several potential issues in the area of taxation. The treatment of revaluation reserves has already been discussed. A related issue is the research grants received. These are treated as tax-free grants and for consolidation purposes are recorded as income, in accordance with IAS and US-GAAP. However, tax is payable if the grants are distributed as dividends to shareholders, but the grants can be used as an offset against losses to avoid taxes. The cumulative amount at December 31, 1992 is Lira 600 billion. No deferred taxation is provided on this amount, which was considered to be acceptable under US-GAAP at that time as no tax is going to be paid directly on this amount. In 1992, a tax on shareholders' equity (a wealth tax) was introduced. The law allows companies to account for this as a reduction of shareholders' equity without going through income. This treatment, adopted by Olivetti, is inconsistent with IAS and US-GAAP. The 1992 charge was Lira 25 billion and this would be a charge to income, with no effect on equity itself.

Another source of potential deferred tax not considered necessary is the so-called "Equalization Tax," which requires the company to pay tax on distributed income if the original income had not been taxed at the maximum corporate rate. This results from the tax imputation system in Italy where individual taxpayers include dividends at the gross (pretax) amounts and then get a credit for taxes paid by the company. While the Italian profession considers this as creating a potential for deferred taxes, Italian and US technical partners believe that any such tax payments are part of the dividends that are paid, so under US-GAAP no deferred tax needs to be provided.

Olivetti has netted off deferred tax assets and liabilities without separately disclosing these amounts. Under SFAS 109, such disclosures would be required for US-GAAP purposes. In addition, there are potential deferred tax assets via the tax loss carryforwards that total Lira 3,700 billion at fiscal year-end 1992, of which Lira 1,000 billion has an infinite useful life. As the system of taxation in Italy is a complex combination of legal entity and group taxation, it is an arduous task to evaluate the likely recovery of all of these losses. However, as the group has recently been reporting operating losses, it is plausible to argue that no deferred tax assets should be created under IAS and US-GAAP.

In 1992, no reconciliation is made to the effective tax rate because of the reported loss. However, details of the sources of taxes paid are provided. As tax loss carryforwards are utilized, a reclassification under US-GAAP would have been necessary as the tax effect of operating losses was shown as extraordinary items prior to SFAS 109.

In sum, the tax question is complex and would require a large effort to ensure that there is full compliance with US-GAAP under SFAS 109. This is not considered to be cost effective for this study, but it is worth noting that no specific tax differences arose for the reconciliations performed through 1989. Consequently, it is the relatively new rules of SFAS 109 that create the potential for differences, and these are likely to be in the area of creating deferred tax assets.

H. Post-Employment Benefits

Olivetti's policy is to accrue for pension or severance obligations using the method applicable within each country. A significant part of operations is in Italy, which has state-based pension and health care systems. A severance payment is due and this is fully accrued based on an assumption that everyone leaves at the fiscal year-end. If it is assumed that real rates of return lead to discount rates greater than rates of salary increase, then this is likely to overstate the present value of the pension obligation for these companies. While it is plausible that there are under-accrued pension obligations, the bulk of activity occurs in other parts of Europe, where defined benefit plans are rare or largely accrued (except perhaps for the impact of future salary increases), and the US, where US-GAAP rules are applied. In 1989, the adjustment to earnings and equity was an increase in both amounts of Lira 4 billion (pretax). Given the immaterial amount in 1989, it was not considered reasonable to calculate any difference at the end of 1992 for the purpose of this study, especially as, given the restructuring since 1989, the adjustment should not exceed the 1989 amount. Other post-employment benefits for reorganization are included in the provision for restructuring. There are no post-retirement health care plans outside the US. There was no material accrual required in 1992 for the US operations. Revised IAS and US-GAAP require additional disclosures in this area.

I. Revenue Recognition

Revenues from rental and technical assistance contracts are recognized "ratably over the contract term." This is based on milestones that should approximate a percentage of completion approach. It was not feasible to quantify any difference, but it was reassuring that there was no reconciling item related to revenue recognition when the reconciliation to US-GAAP was made in 1989.

J. Segment Disclosures

Olivetti arguably operates in one line of business, but it does not disclose geographical segment data for any income measure as required under both IAS and US-GAAP.

K. Related Party Transactions

Olivetti discusses related party transactions and stated that all related party transactions were disclosed. However, US-GAAP requires more detailed disclosures.

L. Statement of Cash Flow

Olivetti provides a statement of changes in financial position reconciling to changes in financial indebtedness. This does not conform to revised IAS 7 nor to US-GAAP.

M. Other Items

Another deferred charge relates to interest incurred while awaiting a low interest loan from the government for certain research. The company and its auditors argue that this was part of the cost of borrowing and is an explicit part of the loan. This is treated as a prepaid interest expense, which may be acceptable under US-GAAP and IAS, which do not differ on such items. As it is an unusual transaction and is not a function of any IAS versus US-GAAP differences, this treatment is accepted for the purposes of this report.

Earnings per share would need to be calculated and disclosed under US-GAAP. There is much discussion of operating activity throughout the report. This information would need to be brought together and expanded under SEC rules in the management discussion and analysis section.

SUMMARY

Olivetti applies Italian GAAP, which incorporates IAS where the local GAAP is silent. The key areas of difference to US-GAAP apply in the areas of accounting for acquisitions, revaluations of assets, and deferred taxes. However, there are also a number of small areas of difference, some of which are peculiar to Italy, many of which will disappear once the revised IAS apply.

B-8 The Valeo Group

OVERVIEW

Valeo S.A. is an independent automotive components manufacturer. It has operations in 15 countries with a concentration in France and other European Community countries, as well as in North and South America and Asia.

Valeo's shares are listed on the Paris Stock Exchange. At December 31, 1992, the fiscal year-end for the annual report used for this analysis, one shareholder, Cerus, held 36.3% of shares outstanding and 40% of the voting rights. No other single shareholder held more than 4% of the shares. Valeo prepares its financial statements "in accordance with" French GAAP and the international accounting principles formulated by the IASC. Where IAS offers options and no French GAAP exists, then Valeo looks to US-GAAP for guidance. Valeo demonstrates how a French company can choose accounting principles consistent with French GAAP and IAS, and minimize differences with US-GAAP.

SPECIFIC DIFFERENCES

A. Acquisitions, Business Combinations, and Consolidations

Valeo does not consolidate all its subsidiaries, but those unconsolidated generally are legal shells; Valeo made assurances that these are immaterial in aggregate with no off-balance sheet or income statement items being held in them. These subsidiaries are classified as long-term investments, and are written down to account for cumulative losses. Thus, they are essentially treated on an equity basis, with adjustments going through other financial expenses. While full consolidation is required under US-GAAP, there will be no effect on the reconciliations to earnings and shareholders' equity if full consolidation occurs because of their immateriality.

Valeo applies equity accounting for most of its associate companies. However, for joint ventures, it applies proportional consolidation, which is the benchmark treatment under IAS. In general, US-GAAP requires use of equity accounting. Applying the equity method to joint ventures has no impact on net income or shareholders' equity, but could have an impact on any components reported separately. The maximum impact will be around one percent, so it is not material. Further, since the publication of the 1992 annual report, the SEC has allowed use of proportional consolidation for non-US registrants.

Goodwill arising from acquisitions is amortized over 20 or 40 years. For all acquisitions made since 1986, goodwill was based on fair value of net assets acquired. Prior to then, there may be some older acquisitions for which the fair value assessment could differ from the requirements of US-GAAP, but the information is not available to make this assessment nor to make any retroactive adjustments. However, given the acquisitions made prior to 1986, management considered it unlikely that there would be any material adjustment. The SEC has been known to be understanding of non-US registrants' inability to reconstruct such data, so no adjustment is likely. The amortization periods are fundamentally consistent with US-GAAP. From 1995, IAS 22 allows a maximum amortization period of 20 years and an annual evaluation of the unamortized balance. However, the revised IAS does not require retroactive adjustments, so no goodwill adjustments appear to be required.

Note 3 in the 1992 annual report details the changes in the goodwill account in conformity with French GAAP. This disclosure is more extensive than under US-GAAP and IAS.

B. Foreign Currency Translation

Valeo adopts the US dollar as the functional currency for the translation of subsidiaries operating in a hyperinflationary economy. Although this treatment seems to be consistent with IAS and the logic laid out in SFAS 52, the SEC has usually chosen to adopt a view that the parent currency (that is, French Franc) should be the functional currency in such situations if the subsidiary invoices its sales in the local currency.

Similarly, Valeo has an associated company accounted for on an equity basis that itself has a subsidiary operating in a hyperinflationary economy. The subsidiary (of the associated company) applies local GAAP and performs price-level adjustments for the tangible assets, which are incorporated into the subsidiary's group accounts at revalued amounts. This is consistent with revised IAS, but not US-GAAP. The total effect on Valeo's income in 1992 is FF40 million, but this does not necessarily reflect the difference for US-GAAP purposes, which require historical costs with remeasurement into a functional currency or the parent currency. The potential difference is not quantifiable as

Valeo does not have access to the detailed information. In December 1994, the SEC accepted this treatment under IAS 21 for non-US registrants.

Foreign currency transactions are translated at the transaction date or hedging rate. This is essentially consistent with IAS and US-GAAP except to the extent that there is a discount or premium at the inception of a hedge (calculated as the difference between the spot and hedged exchange rates). These discounts/premia should be amortized over the life of the contract rather than recognized immediately. Any such difference was not material at December 31, 1992.

C. Shareholders' Equity

Valeo provides a statement of changes in shareholders' equity as required under IAS and US-GAAP.

Valeo issues employee stock options in several years. The employee stock options offered since 1990 were based on a price equal to 90 percent of the fair market value (a 20 trading day average price). The 10-percent benefit to employees was not recognized as compensation as required under US-GAAP. While IAS are silent on the specific issue, it is argued that the Framework permits accrual of the compensation expense. The impact of this accrual (after tax) would be approximately FF2 million on the 1992 income and FF8 million on 1992 shareholders' equity. Neither of these amounts would be material enough to warrant inclusion in a reconciliation to US-GAAP. Further, adequate disclosure is provided to allow one to compute the potential expense.

D. Property, Plant, and Equipment

No specific measurement differences exist, although potential differences could have arisen had Valeo chosen different options under IAS and/or French GAAP. One area of anticipated difference does not occur because the legal revaluations required in France (and some other European countries) are excluded in the consolidated financial statements so that the assets are at historical cost book values, as required under US-GAAP and the benchmark treatment under IAS.

Second, Valeo capitalizes certain lease obligations. It appears that all such leases requiring capitalization under IAS or US-GAAP have been capitalized. However, Valeo does not provide the detailed contractual obligation payment schedule split into operating and capital leases, as required under US-GAAP and recommended under IAS.

Valeo's policy of expensing all research and development costs is consistent with US-GAAP. Certain development expenditures may need to be capitalized from 1995 under the revised IAS. However, there is no retroactive adjustment required and the amounts likely would not be material. There is also no material amount of interest that could have been capitalized under US-GAAP and the alternative approach in revised IAS 23.

E. Investments

All material investments other than in affiliates or associate companies are in bank deposits and are reflected at the lower of cost and market value.

Valeo discloses information of its open positions in forward, option, and swap contracts in more detail than is often found presented by US companies, especially prior to SFAS 105 and 107. However, it does not disclose any net asset or liability arising from these positions.

While the disclosures were consistent with IAS and US-GAAP at December 1992, as the various regulations for financial instruments evolve, increased disclosure will likely occur.

F. Discontinued Operations and Changes in Accounting Policy

Valeo reported discontinued operations and changes in accounting policies in 1990. The discontinued operations would probably not qualify as such under revised IAS and US-GAAP. Further, there would be additional disclosures relating to the change in accounting policy. These are reclassification issues and would not affect the reconciliations to income or shareholders' equity.

G. Income Taxes

The company utilizes a liability method for deferred taxes, based on differences of the tax and accounting values of assets and liabilities. The stated policy is not to recognize deferred tax assets for temporary differences not offset by deferred tax liabilities, unless the realization of the asset is assured by carrybacks. Valeo discloses the potential deferred tax assets of FF422 million, which relates in part to tax loss carryforwards. Given the profitability of the company, and based on discussions with management, a deferred tax asset is recognized.

The tax disclosures are quite detailed but less comprehensive than required under SFAS 109 for current US-GAAP. They were adequate under SFAS 96 under consideration at that time.

An unusual item relates to taxes on dividend distributions arising out of the tax imputation system in France. Note 8.3 of the 1992 financial statements indicates that "Distribution by the parent company of the balance of its retained earnings ... would result in additional tax of FF640 million." However, this tax is considered a payment on behalf of shareholders and is treated as a form of dividend; hence, it is not recorded as an expense of the company. As a result, there is no deferred tax provided for this amount. There appear to be no IAS dealing with this issue, which is considered to be consistent with US-GAAP by Coopers and Lybrand L.L.P.'s technical partners. The major US accounting firms are reevaluating this type of practice in the context of SFAS 109.

H. Post-Employment Benefits

Pension obligations for French employees, to a large extent, are the responsibility of the state. Hence, the firm-specific obligations are not of the same potential magnitude as for a US company. Nevertheless, where the firm and its subsidiaries (for example, in the US) have defined benefit plans, the actuarial calculations are consistent with US-GAAP, including the use of estimated future salary levels. This treatment is consistent with revised IAS, with the possible exception of the use of a long-term interest rate under IAS and a potentially variable rate under US-GAAP. However, this difference is not currently material. The disclosure provided is not as comprehensive as under US-GAAP, but the obligation is accrued except for a small amount for a recently acquired subsidiary for which the obligation (FF16 million) is being accrued over 15 years, as is consistent with US-GAAP and IAS.

   The only other post-employment benefits are for health care obligations in the US subsidiary, which will be fully accrued in 1993; the accrual is immaterial. Post-employment benefits relating to restructuring/reorganization have been accrued. The disclosures required by SFAS 112 were not in effect at the time of the 1992 report.

I. Revenue Recognition

Valeo's practices are consistent with IAS and US-GAAP.

J. Segment Reporting

Valeo provides detailed line-of-business and geographical segment data on net sales; net property, plant, and equipment; and capital expenditure. But no income measure is reported on a segment basis. This treatment is not consistent with either US-GAAP or IAS. The company is uncomfortable with presenting these disclosures because of perceived competitive disadvantages.

K. Related Party Transactions

Management indicated that all such transactions were disclosed.

L. Statement of Cash Flows

Valeo's statement of cash flows is largely consistent with IAS and US-GAAP, except that it includes short-term debt (up to 12 months maturity) in cash and equivalents. In addition, Valeo does not disclose the details of its change in working capital components, nor does it disclose the actual cash amounts related to interest and taxation as required under IAS and US-GAAP.

M. Other Items

SEC regulations require a management discussion and analysis section with certain prescribed disclosures. This is not required by the FASB or IAS and is not provided by Valeo. Valeo does disclose the impact of a subsequent event as required by US-GAAP and IAS. Additional disclosures on the calculation of earnings per share will also be required.

SUMMARY

Valeo has chosen accounting policies under French GAAP and IAS, which largely comply with US-GAAP. The most significant differences arise in the nonaccrual of deferred tax assets and in the disclosures provided. The disclosures are less complete than required by US-GAAP, and to a lesser extent IAS, notably in the areas of leases, pensions, segment income, and taxation.

References

Acher, G. "The 'Last Chance Saloon' for Judgment." *Financial Times* (January 13, 1995): VIII.

Advisory Panel on Auditor Independence, *Strengthing the Professionalism of the Independent Auditor,* Report to the Public Oversight Board, (1994).

Amir, E., T.S. Harris and E.K. Venuti. "A Comparison of the Value-Relevance of U.S. versus Non-U.S. GAAP Accounting Measures Using Form 20-F Reconciliations." *Journal of Accounting Research* (Supplement 1993): 230-64.

Barth, M.E. and G. Clinch. "International Accounting Differences and Their Relation to Share Prices: Evidence from U.K., Australian, and Canadian Firms." Working paper, Harvard University, May 1994.

Beese, J.C. Jr. "A Rule That Stunts Growth" *The Wall Street Journal,* (February 8, 1994): A18.

Breeden, R.C. "Foreign Companies and U.S. Securities Markets in a Time of Economic Transformation." *Fordham International Law Journal,* Vol 17 (1994): S77-96.

Choi, F.D.S. and Lee, C. "Merger Premia and National Differences in Accounting for Goodwill" *Journal of International Financial Management and Accounting* (Autumn 1991): 219-240.

Cochrane, J.L. "Are U.S. Regulatory Requirements for Foreign Firms Appropriate?" *Fordham International Law Journal,* Vol 17 (1994): S58-67.

Decker, W.E. "The Attractions of the U.S. Securities Markets to Foreign Issuers and the Alternative Methods of Accessing the U.S. Markets: From the Issuer's Perspective." *Fordham International Law Journal,* Vol 17 (1994): S10-24.

Easton, P.D., P.H. Eddey and T.S. Harris. "An Investigation of Revaluations of Tangible Long-Lived Assets." *Journal of Accounting Research* (Supplement 1993): 1-38.

Edwards, F.R. "Listing of Foreign Securities on U.S. Exchanges." in *Modernizing U.S. Securities Regulation: Economic and Legal Perspectives,* edited by K. Lehn and R.W. Kamphuis Jr., University of Pittsburgh (1992): 53-70.

Fuerbringer, J. "S.E.C. Says No on German Stocks." *New York Times* (April 26, 1992).

Greene, E.F., D.A. Braverman and S.R. Sperber. "Internationalization of the World's Capital Markets: U.S. Regulatory Alternatives." Working paper, Cleary, Gottlieb, Steen & Hamilton, 1994.

Harris, T.S. *Understanding German Financial Statements: Lessons From Daimler-Benz's Listing.* Salomon Brothers, October 7, 1993.

Harris, T.S., M. Lang and H.P. Möller. "The Value Relevance of German Accounting Measures: An Empirical Analysis." *Journal of Accounting Research* (Autumn 1994): 187-209.

Herz, R.H. "Accounting and Financial Reporting for Derivatives and Synthetics." in *The Handbook of Derivatives & Synthetics*, edited by R.A. Klein and J. Lederman. Probus Publishing (1994): 821-875.

Knutson, P.H. *Financial Reporting in the 1990s and Beyond.* Association for Investment Management and Research (1993).

Liener, G. "Accounting Standards Required for Global Corporations by the International Capital Markets - Consequences for the German Consolidated Financial Statements." Speech presented at *Global Capital Raising* Forum Düsseldorf, March 9, 1994.

Velli, J. "American Depositary Receipts: An Overview." *Fordham International Law Journal*, Vol 17 (1994): S38-57.

Index